Thomas Cook **pocket** guides

HONG KONG

Written by Helena Zukowski
Updated by Nicola Churchouse

Published by Thomas Cook Publishing
A division of Thomas Cook Tour Operations Limited
Company registration no. 3772199 England
The Thomas Cook Business Park, Unit 9, Coningsby Road,
Peterborough PE3 8SB, United Kingdom
Email: books@thomascook.com, Tel: +44 (0) 1733 416477
www.thomascookpublishing.com

Produced by Cambridge Publishing Management Limited
Burr Elm Court, Main Street, Caldecote CB23 7NU
www.cambridgepm.co.uk

ISBN: 978-1-84848-333-0

© 2006, 2008 Thomas Cook Publishing
This third edition © 2010 Thomas Cook Publishing
Text © Thomas Cook Publishing
Maps © Thomas Cook Publishing/PCGraphics (UK) Limited
Transport map © Communicarta Limited

Series Editor: Karen Beaulah
Production/DTP: Steven Collins

Printed and bound in Spain by GraphyCems

Cover photography: © Jo Miyake/Alamy

CONTENTS

INTRODUCING HONG KONG

Introduction 6

When to go 8

The International
   Dragon Boat Festival 14

History 16

Lifestyle 18

Culture 20

**MAKING THE MOST OF
HONG KONG**

Shopping 24

Eating & drinking 26

Entertainment & nightlife 30

Sport & relaxation 34

Accommodation 36

The best of Hong Kong 42

Suggested itineraries 44

Something for nothing 46

When it rains 48

On arrival 50

THE CITY OF HONG KONG

Hong Kong Island 62

Kowloon 78

New Territories 94

OUT OF TOWN

The Outer Islands 106

Further afield
   (Macau & Shenzhen) 122

PRACTICAL INFORMATION

Directory 144

Emergencies 154

INDEX 156

MAPS

Hong Kong 52

Hong Kong transport 56

Hong Kong Island 63

Kowloon 79

New Territories 95

Outer Islands 107

Macau 123

SYMBOLS KEY

The following symbols are used throughout this book:

ⓐ address ☎ telephone ⓦ website address ⓔ email
🕔 opening times Ⓝ public transport connections ❶ important

The following symbols are used on the maps:

𝒊	information office	▪	POI (point of interest)
✈	airport	○	city
✚	hospital	○	large town
🛡	police station	○	small town
🚌	bus station	═	motorway
🚆	railway station	—	main road
Ⓜ	metro		minor road
✝	cathedral	—	railway
❶	numbers denote featured cafés & restaurants		

Hotels and restaurants are graded by approximate price as follows:
£ budget price **££** mid-range price **£££** expensive

▶ *The Central District is the financial hub of Hong Kong*

INTRODUCING
Hong Kong

Introduction

At first sight, Hong Kong is like a huge pinball machine sitting by the sea – flashy, always on the move, all lights and action, a gambler's stab at the good life. It has been described to the point of cliché as a seamless blend of East and West, more modern than tomorrow but firmly anchored in ancient Chinese wisdom. Yet scratch below the surface and the cliché falls apart, for no other city titillates the senses to such a degree or throws out such a bewildering set of contradictions.

Look around and you'll see the ultimate in modern architecture and technology beside rundown tenement buildings, age-old junks in the harbour next to sleek cruise ships. You can eat at restaurants that would outclass many in New York or slurp soup on the pavement at a *dai pai dong* (licensed mobile food stall); spend the day hiking in the remote, unspoilt peaks of the New Territories then party all night long at wine bars, jazz clubs or good old-fashioned pubs back in the heart of town.

Even for those who've watched Hong Kong grow and change over many decades, the city never loses its fascination. The ride across the 'fragrant harbour' (for this is what Hong Kong means) from Kowloon to Hong Kong Island on the Star Ferry will always be tinged with romance. The view from Victoria Peak will explain why Hong Kong is often called one of the five most beautifully situated cities in the world. Most of all, despite the crowds, the pollution, the jostling, there is a profound admiration for a people who have the powerful capacity to persevere and endure. Since its birth, Hong Kong has been hit with setbacks from all directions – from economic depression to internal protests and health scares – and has bounced back stronger and more glamorous every time.

In Chinese mythology, the phoenix bird appears rarely but signals the birth of a new era. It hasn't been reported, but in all likelihood, a beautiful red bird is watching over Fragrant Harbour.

⬤ *The old and the new sit side by side in Hong Kong*

When to go

As long as you're not put off by seasonal humidity (see below), Hong Kong is a great city to visit at any time of year.

SEASONS & CLIMATE

Hong Kong is subtropical but still has its seasons. Spring (from March to mid-May) is warm but the humidity can be high and fog and drizzle often dampen the comfort level. Temperatures range from 18°C to 27°C (64–80°F) with an 82 per cent humidity. While days are warm, evenings can be cool enough for a lightweight jacket.

Summer (late May to mid-September) tends to be hot and humid with sweltering heat during midsummer, so sightseeing can be a sweaty affair. This is also the rainy season, and warm but torrential downpours often occur. Temperatures range upwards from 33°C (91°F), with humidity near 86 per cent. Short-sleeved cotton shirts are best, with a lightweight sweater to cope with heavily air-conditioned restaurants. Don't forget an umbrella – for rain or shine.

September brings a special problem – typhoons – and the threat seems to loom all month. From late September to early December the temperatures and humidity drop and days are clear and sunny; these are the best months to visit. Temperatures range from 18°C to 28°C (64–82°F) and the humidity is 72 per cent. Temperatures cool down in the winter (from mid-December to February) and nights can be quite chilly. It's a good idea to bring woollens and overcoats to cope with temperature swings.

ANNUAL EVENTS

Hong Kong is a city that loves to celebrate, so you're likely to find something festive happening all year round. Since dates vary,

it's a good idea to check with the Hong Kong Tourism Board
(see page 152) for a complete list if you want to enjoy the fun.

January & February

Chinese New Year (3 Feb 2011; 23 Jan 2012) Hong Kong grinds to
a virtual standstill for what is the most important holiday of the
Chinese calendar. Many shops close for three days; there's a huge
street parade on the first day, fireworks on the second and one of
the largest horse races of the year in Sha Tin on the third.

◆ *Traditional dragon dances greet the Chinese New Year*

● *In the starting blocks for the Hong Kong Marathon*

February
Hong Kong Marathon Serious athletes and fun-runners at least start together, while everybody else seems to turn out to spectate. Ⓦ www.hkmarathon.com

February & March
The Hong Kong Arts Festival For almost two months, the city swells with opera, jazz, classical music, theatre and dance performed by artists from around the globe. Ⓦ www.artsfestival.org

March & April

Hong Kong Sevens The city turns into rugby (union) lovers' heaven at the 40,000-seat Hong Kong Stadium. ⓦ www.hksevens.com

The Hong Kong International Film Festival A two-week film indulgence screening some 300 titles from around the world. ⓦ www.hkiff.org.hk

May

Cheung Chau Bun Festival The week-long festival honours the god Pak Tai, whose 200-year-old temple is dedicated to the protection of fishermen. Three 20-m (66-ft) towers are covered with freshly baked sacred buns as an appeasement to the spirits of people killed by pirates. One of the festival's highlights is a parade where colourfully dressed children seem to float through the air, an illusion created by cleverly designed supports.

May & June

The International Dragon Boat Festival One-day carnivals, with dragon boat regattas, junk parties and fairs, are held on several beaches around Hong Kong (see pages 14–15).

July & August

Ani-Com Hong Kong (late July & early Aug) Not just animation products and comics, but cosplay and computer games, too, at the Hong Kong Convention & Exhibition Centre (see page 76). ⓦ www.ani-com.hk

August

Hungry Ghosts Festival When the gates of hell are believed to open, releasing 'hungry ghosts' to walk on earth for two weeks.

Throughout the festival, offerings are burned and food is set out for the spirits.

September
Mid-Autumn Festival (12 Sept 2011; 30 Sept 2012) Held on the fifteenth night of the eighth moon, the festival remembers an

◯ *Massive towers of sweet buns feature in the Cheung Chau Bun Festival*

uprising against the Mongols in the 14th century. Lanterns are lit, special pastries known as 'mooncakes' are eaten and a spectacular fire dragon dance takes place in Tai Hang, near Causeway Bay.

November & December
Hong Kong Winterfest From the end of November to December, the skyscrapers on either side of the harbour are glammed up with festive lights and downtown Hong Kong is transformed into a winter wonderland complete with 'Santa Town'.

PUBLIC HOLIDAYS
New Year's Day 1 Jan
Lunar New Year 3–5 Feb 2011; 23–25 Jan 2012
Ching Ming Festival (Ancestral Remembrance) 5 Apr 2011; 4 Apr 2012
Good Friday 22 Apr 2011; 6 Apr 2012
Day after Good Friday 23 Apr 2011; 7 Apr 2012
Easter Monday 25 Apr 2011; 9 Apr 2012
Labour Day 1 May
Buddha's Birthday 10 May 2011; 28 May 2012
International Dragon Boat Festival 6 June 2011; 23 June 2012
Hong Kong SAR Establishment Day 1 July
Day after Mid-Autumn Festival 13 Sept 2011; 1 Oct 2012
National Day 1 Oct
Chung Yeung Festival (Ancestral Remembrance) 5 Oct 2011; 23 Oct 2012
Christmas Day 25 Dec
Boxing Day 26 Dec

The International Dragon Boat Festival

The International Dragon Boat Festival is without a doubt one of Hong Kong's biggest sporting and social events of the year. What's particularly appealing about it is that there's something for everyone. Residents – both local and expat – form teams to compete in dragon boat races, families make a day of the beach fairs and colourful happenings, and party animals scamper from one junk to another, imbibing everything in sight. What's more, the weather is usually at its best: just warm enough for you to appreciate a cold drink, but not so hot that your skin will sizzle.

Historically, the event honours the death of a man of scrupulous beliefs who threw himself into a river to protest against corrupt government. He was so loved and admired by the common folk that fishermen rushed out in long boats to retrieve his body, beating drums to scare the fish away and throwing rice dumplings into the water for any remaining fish that didn't get the hint.

Dragon boat racing is taken seriously in Hong Kong. Teams train for months prior to the event and much friendly rivalry goes on, especially between participants from rival multinationals. While dragon boat festivals are held in several other areas such as Lamma (see pages 118–21) and Lantau (see pages 108–14), the biggest by far is usually the one on Stanley Beach, on the south side of the Island.

Regatta days are like carnivals, with the races forming the backdrop to a frenzy of eating, drinking and playing. Spectators picnic on the beach, while those in the know – or with connections – hop aboard one of the corporate-sponsored junks moored in the bay. Food and drink stalls abound, ideal for snacking through the afternoon. The atmosphere is infectious, with the constant thumping of the dragon boat drums, splashing of the water and ever-louder cheering. Even

▲ *Dragon boat races are hotly contested*

after the races have come to their nail-biting conclusion, the party still continues for those who want it to.

The festival is actually on the fifth day of the fifth month of the lunar calendar, which means that the dragon boat season is usually in May or June. The **Stanley Dragon Boat Association** provides more information at Ⓦ www.dragonboat.org.hk. Smaller-scale events are also held in Discovery Bay, Lantau, and on Tai Wan To Beach on Lamma Island (see Ⓦ www.lammadragonboat.com for details of the latter).

History

Even though Hong Kong's story goes back thousands of years, historians usually begin just 150 years ago, when Britain and China, then already trading partners, hit an impasse over the cost of silk and tea. During the 1800s, tea had become the British national drink and the only place it was grown was China. Similarly, silk was highly prized and China was the sole producer. Britain tried to encourage the Chinese to buy British goods, but they would have none of it: all they wanted was silver bullion in payment for silk and tea. The Chinese also forbade anyone to enter their kingdom with the exception of a small trading depot at Canton.

As frustration built, the British traders found one thing the Chinese would buy, albeit secretly – Indian-grown opium. Before long, silver was flowing in the opposite direction as Chinese of all classes became enslaved to the drug. In retaliation, the Chinese emperor declared a ban on opium importing, but the British continued to smuggle it in. In 1839, the Chinese hit back by burning all supplies of opium stockpiled in Canton, thereby launching the first Opium War. However, Chinese war junks were no match for the Royal Navy and in humiliation the Chinese had to sign the Treaty of Nanking, which allowed the continued importation of opium and ceded Hong Kong Island in perpetuity to Britain. In the second Opium War (1856–60) Kowloon was added, and then the New Territories in 1898 on a 99-year lease.

Over the next century, Hong Kong's unique blend of Chinese life and British traditions developed and the economy flourished under an appointed governing body. As the lease began to run out, China launched a series of talks to define a new way of governing Hong Kong, which was to return to China as a Special Administrative

Region (SAR), guaranteeing its capitalist lifestyle and social system for at least 50 years after 1997.

Since the handover, Hong Kong has encountered localised bumps and difficulties, as well as problems generated further afield. The city was hit hard by the Asian financial crisis of 1997–98, and again by the global economic collapse of 2007, but has bounced back each time with renewed vigour. There have also been political difficulties in trying to reconcile Communist policies with Hong Kong's desire for economic freedom. One of the most serious threats to the area was the eruption of SARS in 2003 – the mysterious, flu-like ailment; this dealt a major blow to the Hong Kong economy, hitting retail trade, business and tourism. But more than a decade after it reverted to Chinese rule, life in Hong Kong has not changed greatly. The economy is booming again, tourism is thriving, and the city is still synonymous with working hard and playing even harder.

Hong Kong has always thrived on spirit and tenacity and, as we move into the second decade of the 21st century, that special Hong Kong energy shows no signs of fading.

⬥ Hong Kong's coastal location has been critical to its history

Lifestyle

If there's any one golden ideal in Hong Kong it's the dream of rising from rags to riches, for this is a city that fairly abounds in tales of entrepreneurs who created empires from scratch. People work very hard in Hong Kong – all part of an obsession they have with success. Immigrants share one dream: to make money quickly. So everything seems to move at lightning speed.

When they do take a break, Hong Kongers seem to play with the same feverish intensity – whether it's betting on the horses or playing cricket. Dining together is one of their favourite pursuits, but if you're invited to dinner it's highly unlikely it will be to your host's home. Most flats here are very small so social entertaining is usually at restaurants. These gatherings tend to be at large round tables in vast, noisy establishments, where the food comes in relays and everyone shares. Ordering your own dish (as is common in the West) would be unthinkable.

Lunches downtown are usually taken in a hurry and are a bit of a feeding frenzy. But this is just Hong Kong dining, and after a while most visitors are seduced.

While Western traditions are everywhere, superstitions still weave through daily life. Take a stroll through the Temple Street Night Market (see page 82) and you'll see Hong Kongers seated at small tables listening intently as fortune-tellers read their palms or consult their cards. The Chinese take all this very seriously and will tell you that palm reading, fortune sticks, facial reading and other methods of future prediction go way back in time. The Chinese zodiac is consulted when young couples plan a family, since being born or married in a particular year can determine the whole course of a child's life. Perhaps the most persuasive belief is in feng shui ('wind and water'), based on the belief that wind and water were created by the gods and therefore reflect their will. It influences where parks are placed, tunnels dug, highways carved out, buildings located and even where graves are sited.

◆ *Early morning tai chi in one of the parks*

Culture

Although Westerners may initially feel at home in Hong Kong, after a while they will realise that it is rooted in a very ancient Chinese tradition. (The population is 95 per cent Chinese, with the vast majority being Cantonese.)

Even though Hong Kong is a modern, capitalist society, it still holds strongly to the paternalistic, family-oriented system established by China's most venerable sage, Confucius. He believed that all individuals are directly responsible for their fate, so a person should always think carefully before acting. With this kind of grounding, little wonder the Chinese have the work ethic they do along with traditional values that include respect for elders, reverence for ancestors and a belief in perseverance.

Within the family, parents will work extremely long hours to ensure their children get the best in healthcare and education so that one day they will look after their parents in their old age. Children grow up expecting to support their parents and to honour their ancestors by regularly visiting their graves and making offerings. Unlike in the West, overt affection is not usually displayed; love and caring are expressed through acts of kindness, not words.

The lives of young people in Hong Kong are quite different from their Western counterparts. Since the cost of accommodation is high, they tend to live at home until they marry, and often even after marriage the couple continue living with parents. When they're courting, it is highly unlikely couples will be without siblings or relatives watching. The only romantic retreats are public parks. For those who need undisturbed passion, 'love motels' can be rented by the hour.

🔻 *Chinese opera is a colourful and exciting spectacle*

While it may appear that money is the major god worshipped in Hong Kong, religion does continue to play a big role in people's lives. Most are either Buddhist or Taoist with about 500,000 Christians and a handful of Muslims, Hindus, Sikhs and Jews. Throughout Hong Kong you will see people lighting incense at temple shrines or visiting ornate monasteries where nuns and monks are supported. Unlike mainland China's ban on certain new religious movements such as the Falun Gong and Xiantianism, Hong Kong enjoys total freedom of religious practice.

While Western medicine is routinely practised, Chinese herbal medicine still remains popular and is surprisingly effective for universal complaints such as the common cold, 'flu, chronic backache, asthma and migraine headaches. Chinese medicine dates back 5,000 years and a visit to a Chinese herbalist is an enlightening experience. The herbalist will pull out of a battery of tiny drawers in a huge wall cupboard a wild assortment of powders, twigs and dried objects, and instruct you on how to prepare the cure. (You really don't want to know what you've been given, but the mixture often works like a charm.)

Chinese acupuncture is a common treatment in the West – especially for soft tissue injuries. In Hong Kong, it's used to treat long-term complaints by – according to the acupuncturist – using energy channels or meridians from the point of insertion to the area of complaint.

◗ *View of the city from Victoria Peak*

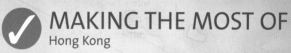

MAKING THE MOST OF
Hong Kong

Shopping

Hong Kong is a shopaholic's paradise, but even those with a lower threshold for retail therapy are likely to find something to buy. Some of the best items are clothing, high-tech goodies, electronics, jewellery, pearls, watches, spectacles and silk sheets. Credit cards are widely accepted (except in the markets).

THE BESPOKE BUBBLE

One of the many Hong Kong stories that refuses to die is that of bargain-priced suits tailored to perfection in just 24 hours. Perhaps the myth survives because if you shop around you can still find suits made in a day – although you wouldn't want to wear the end result in public.

The legend began in the 1950s when escapees from Shanghai, many of them tailors accustomed to stitching up quality garments, flooded into Hong Kong. Later, during the Korean and Vietnam wars, US soldiers coming through Hong Kong on R&R flocked to tailor shops looking for cheap, custom-made suits. Before long, English-speaking South Asians with tailoring experience were appearing all over Tsim Sha Tsui, catering to military personnel, tourists and local business people. Competition and cheap labour from the mainland bred Hong Kong's high-quality, low-price reputation and gave birth to the cheap 24-hour suit.

Today, a well-tailored garment in Hong Kong will cost as much as back home, but with a difference – the quality of the fit. A good suit today will take a minimum of three days and two fittings.

The main shopping areas are Central and Causeway Bay on Hong Kong Island and Tsim Sha Tsui and Mong Kok in Kowloon. Many of the low-end clothing outlets and department stores are in Causeway Bay and there are warehouse sales, factory extras outlets and cheap jeans in Lee Garden Road. The best places for designer fashions are the shopping centres, and the new outlet mall at Tung Chung.

For browsers, budget shoppers and those who are just interested in people-watching, the best places to start are Hong Kong's many open-air or covered markets. The biggest in the territory is the Temple Street Night Market (see page 82) in Yau Ma Tei for cheap clothes, knock-off watches, pirated CDs and DVDs, footwear and cookware. It's a good place to sample street food and perhaps visit one of the many fortune-tellers who lay bare your future with the assistance of a trained bird. Stanley Market on the southern part of Hong Kong Island is as much a tourist destination as a place to shop, but it also has lots of good clothing bargains – including cashmere sweaters, good-quality linen clothing and rock-bottom-priced pashminas.

Even though the city isn't the total bargain basement it once was, there are no sales taxes and shops offer great buys – particularly for anyone who likes to bargain. And you can haggle over price anywhere, except in department stores where prices are fixed. Those coming mainly to shop should visit during end-of-season sales (January to February and July to August) when prices are slashed.

Just a few words of advice: don't buy anything in a hurry and always shop around to compare prices. Be sure electronic items and cameras come with at least a one-year worldwide warranty and that all the accessories said to be included are in the box. If you want to buy authentic goods, particularly antiques and other hard-to-verify items, shop in places where the HKTB logo is clearly displayed.

Eating & drinking

As a popular local saying goes: 'The Chinese eat everything with legs and wings except tables and planes.' And it's true: Chinese cuisine utilises everything that is vaguely edible and creatively spins it into a huge variety of regional styles that range from the subtle flavours of Guangzhou (Canton) to the chilli-laden stir-fries of Sichuan. Traditional Hong Kong food tends to be in the Cantonese style, and with the myriad Western culinary influences in the city, this is also where you'll find some of the most inventive fusion food in the world.

Cantonese food is subtle with delicate, well-balanced flavours, neither salty nor greasy, and prepared by quick stir-frying and steaming. Typical dishes are *xiu ab* (roast duck, seasoned with spices and basted in honey, soy and vinegar), *dung gua ton* (winter melon soup) and the universally loved *dim sum*.

Shantou (Chui Chow) cuisine reflects a love of seafood with dishes such as the controversial *hai ji yu chi ton* (shark's fin soup) and exotic birds'-nest soup. Typical dishes include *chui jau yu ton* (aromatic fish soup) and *chui jau lou sui ngoh* (soyed goose).

East Coast or Shanghai cuisine tends to be strongly flavoured and is usually stewed, fried or braised with a salty taste balanced by sweet flavours. Typical dishes include hot-and-sour soup, drunken chicken (chicken marinated in rice wine) and braised eel.

PRICE CATEGORIES

The following price ratings used throughout this book indicate the average price of a three-course meal for one without drinks.

£ under HK$150   ££ HK$150–300   £££ over HK$300

One of the cuisine's most famous dishes is hairy crab, a delicacy that is usually found only in autumn.

Rich, succulent Beijing cuisine is historically influenced by the Imperial Court and its most famous dish is *bak ging tin ab* (Peking duck). This cuisine uses strongly flavoured vegetables with lots of noodles, dumplings and bread instead of rice.

Sesame and chilli oil are common flavourings in Sichuan cuisine, which is the most spicy. Star anise, fennel, chilli, coriander and garlic add zip to dishes that blend the five key flavours: sweet, sour, salty, peppery and chilli hot. Some of the culinary treasures are *ma po deo fu* (grandmother's tofu) and *jeung cha ab* (duck smoked in camphor tea).

Hong Kongers love to eat and they have as many places (over 10,000 restaurants in the city) in which to indulge this favourite pastime as dishes to choose from. Some of the best and oldest

▲ *For a novel location try Jumbo, the famous floating restaurant (see page 66)*

restaurants are in major hotels. 'Concept restaurants' abound: some of these – such as **Finds** (ⓐ 2/F Lan Kwai Fong Tower, 33 Wyndham Street, Central ⓞ 2522 9318), which serves light Scandinavian food surrounded by faux igloo walls and chandeliers made of icicles – are a far cry from what you might expect in the heart of Asia. If you are looking for a taste of local culture as well as grub, the *dai pai dong* (licensed mobile food stalls) are great for an alfresco dining experience. These stalls mainly appear after dark in places like the Temple Street Night Market (see page 82). Most sell seafood such as fresh oyster omelette with spring onion and coriander. Some of the *dai pai dong* have moved indoors such as on the east end of Lockhart Road in Wan Chai. There is a cluster of seafood eateries here, open till the early hours of the morning, where the *laat jiu hai* (chilli crab) will make you weep for joy.

More recently, 'private kitchens' have become popular. These are small, unlicensed restaurants, usually unmarked and hidden away. The atmosphere is cosy, the food home-cooked and whatever the chef feels like serving up. While some are hole-in-the-wall joints, many equal their upmarket peers in terms of décor, hygiene and service. There are well over a hundred private kitchens across Hong Kong serving a variety of cuisines. Reservations are a must and the best way to find one is by word of mouth or an Internet search.

You could spend a small fortune at **Gaddi's** (ⓞ 2315 3171) in the Peninsula Hong Kong (see page 38), or eat cheaply where the ordinary folk dine. Places like Tsim Chai Kee Noodle (see page 71) are filled with locals slurping up wonderful noodle soup, fried rice or veggie dishes. Noodle and congee shops are everywhere and serve belly-warming *juk* (rice porridge), or filling helpings of chicken soup thick with noodles. *Dim sum* houses have been around for 1,000 years and eating in them is as much an event as a meal – you pick whatever

THE RULES: DOS & DON'TS

Do ...

- place your chopsticks horizontally on the plate or table, not on your bowl
- spit out your bones or shells on to the table when eating fish or shellfish
- shovel your rice from your bowl instead of picking up rice grains with chopsticks
- say 'thank you' if someone puts food into your bowl
- stand up and lean over the table to get a bit of food on the other side.

Don't ...

- hold your chopsticks pointing straight up or point at anyone (it's very unlucky)
- fill your own tea cup before filling those of fellow diners
- take food from the main plate and put it directly in your mouth (put it in your bowl first)
- flip a whole fish over to get at the other side (it's unlucky as it symbolises the capsizing of a boat)
- start cleaning the table while others are still eating
- pick your teeth without covering your mouth.

you fancy from endless trolleys of hot steamed buns, tarts, puddings, spring rolls and dumplings being pushed past your table. One of the best places to experience the authentic Hong Kong variety is **City Hall Maxim's Palace** (ⓐ 2/F, Low Block, City Hall ☎ 2521 1303), although be warned that the weekend queues sometimes mean a wait of up to 90 minutes if you go at peak times.

Entertainment & nightlife

Hong Kongers tend to carry their 'work hard' ethic into playtime, so there's no end of things to do after dark – from wine bars and dance clubs to Cantonese opera and avant-garde theatre. Many headliners, both high- and low-brow, include Hong Kong on their circuit. A good place for some stand-up comedy is the **Punchline Comedy Club** (❶ 2827 7777 Ⓦ www.punchlinecomedy.com), which often has top international acts performing. Other night-time activities include tours by boat or bus, horse racing at Happy Valley (see page 34), or romantic strolls at the top of Victoria Peak (see page 66) or along the promenade of the Tsim Sha Tsui waterfront. For night-time colour, the Temple Street Night Market (see page 82) and the Ladies' Market (see page 80) near the Mong Kok MTR station are often open until after 22.00.

The once wicked world of Suzie Wong may have faded into history, but there's still more than enough energy and edge to make things lively. Choose from the endless number of sophisticated piano bars, smoky jazz dens, elegant lounges, superstrobe discos and rowdy pubs (many of which don't really take off until after 24.00) and party till dawn before grabbing breakfast and finally tumbling into bed. Most clubs and discos will levy a cover charge, but this usually includes a complimentary drink.

In Central, the happening area is Lan Kwai Fong (also known as the Fong, or LKF) – a narrow alleyway that runs south from D'Aguilar Street and then doglegs west. Once home to rats and tenement housing, LKF has had a facelift and is now the hottest and trendiest place in town, attracting celebs and the young and hip who have cash to spare with its funky music and good food. Trendsetters also like nearby Wyndham Street for its über-cool clubs and the SoHo

⬥ The streets are busy both day and night

WHAT'S ON

It's best to pick up a copy of the free, youth-oriented *HK Magazine*, which lists everything that's going on. It's available at shops, restaurants, hotels and bars. Alternatively, check Ⓦ www.hk-magazine or Ⓦ www.timeout.com.hk

What's On–Hong Kong is a leaflet published weekly by the HKTB listing what's happening in theatre, music and the arts, and distributed at tourist information centres. For special events and nightlife info, check *The List*, *Where Hong Kong*, *CityLife* and *bc* – four free magazines published monthly.

(South of Hollywood Road) district (along the Central/Mid-Levels Escalator), which continues to spawn upmarket ethnic eateries and bars. On weekend nights, Wan Chai is thick with partygoers, and many of the clubs, such as the tacky-but-fun **Strawberry Café Disco** (Ⓐ 48 Hennessy Road, Wan Chai Ⓣ 2866 1031), stay open past dawn every day of the week.

The pubs and bars in Causeway Bay are relatively tame compared with Wan Chai and LKF and there is a handful of bars in Quarry Bay around Tong Chong Street. Kowloon's night scene is more rundown than Central, but places along Knutsford Terrace make a claim to be Kowloon's Lan Kwai Fong. For full details, check Ⓦ www.hkclubbing.com

Hong Kong has over 60 cinemas – mostly multiplexes – that show a mixture of Hollywood blockbusters and local films with English subtitles. Films generally tend to be screened in their original language (so all the Hollywood films are in English), with subtitles in either English or Cantonese. The *South China Morning*

Post and *HK Magazine* list what's currently being shown, which language it's in, and booking information.

To book tickets for cultural events, contact **Urbtix** (☎ 2111 5999 or check ⓦ www.urbtix.hk). Urbtix also has windows at the HK City Hall, the HK Cultural Centre (see page 93), many Tom Lee Music Stores and selected theatres and town halls. A full list of outlets can be found on the website. An hour before any performance, tickets are only available at the box office.

◢ *The buzzing nightlife on Knutsford Terrace*

Sport & relaxation

SPECTATOR SPORTS

Golf The annual highlight is the **Hong Kong Open** (organised by the
Hong Kong Golf Association (ⓦ www.hkga.com), which is held every
November at the Hong Kong Golf Club course.
Hong Kong Golf Club ❸ Lot No 1, Fan Kam Road, Sheung Shui
❶ 2670 1211

Horse racing Hong Kongers love racing, and Happy Valley is the place
to be, though the track in Sha Tin in the New Territories is another
big draw. Races take place Wednesday evenings and some Saturday
and Sunday afternoons from September until June. As racing is the
only legal form of gambling here, the betting is frenzied.
Hong Kong Jockey Club ⓦ www.hkjc.com

● *Soak up the atmosphere at the huge Sha Tin Racecourse*

Sevens Rugby The seven-a-side rugby tournament (called The Sevens, see ⓦ www.hksevens.com), held in March or April at the Hong Kong Stadium, is probably the most popular annual sporting event, drawing in visitors from all over the world.

Hong Kong Stadium ⓐ 55 Eastern Hospital Road, So Kon Po ❶ 2895 7926 ⓦ www.lcsd.gov.hk/stadium

PARTICIPATION SPORTS

Jogging The best jogging trails are Victoria Park's track in Causeway Bay, Bowen Road, Harlech Road and the inside track at Happy Valley – that is if the horses aren't using it. Kowloon Park and the waterfront promenade along Tsim Sha Tsui and Tsim Sha Tsui East are also good.

Marathons There are several marathons, such as the Hong Kong Marathon (February, see page 10) and the China Coast Marathon (January).

RELAXATION

Tai chi Hong Kong is the place to make tai chi, the ancient Chinese regimen designed to balance body and soul, part of your daily life. Both young and older practitioners meet every morning in downtown parks and open spaces to go through the languid motions – and visitors are encouraged to join in.

Every Monday, Wednesday, Thursday and Friday at 08.00 and Saturday at 09.00, you can take a free one-hour lesson (in English) courtesy of the HKTB (see page 152). Weekday classes are at the Sculpture Court in front of the Hong Kong Museum of Art in Tsim Sha Tsui (see pages 83–4). Saturday classes are at the Peak Tower Sky Terrace (see page 66). Visitors must register at the Information Counter on the ground floor of the Peak Tower. Further details from the HKTB.

Accommodation

The cost of a roof over your head is higher in Hong Kong than in many Asian cities, but not as costly as Europe. To get the price range you want, you should always book well in advance – especially if you plan to travel between March and April, and October and November. Major trade fairs at Hong Kong's expanded convention centre also gobble up hotel rooms at various times of the year.

You can book in advance using an Internet hotel agency such as Ⓦ www.expedia.com, Ⓦ www.travelocity.com, Ⓦ www.hotels.com, Ⓦ www.asiatravel.com, Ⓦ www.asiahotels.com and Ⓦ www.quik book.com. It's important to shop around and compare rates at the **Hong Kong Hotels Association** website (Ⓦ www.hkha.com.hk) or individual hotel websites. If you arrive without a place to bed down, contact the Hong Kong Hotels Association on ☎ 2383 8380 or check the reservation centres inside the buffer halls at either Exit A or B of Hong Kong International Airport. They can book you into mid-range to top hotels at great savings.

HOTELS & GUESTHOUSES
Bishop Lei International House £–££ In a residential area popular with expats, a short walk from restaurants and bars, the small rooms are offset by some fine harbour views. ➌ 4 Robinson Road, Mid-Levels

PRICE CATEGORIES
Hotels in this book are graded according to the average price for a double room per night.
£ under HK$1,250   ££ HK$1,250–2,250   £££ over HK$2,250

☎ 2868 0828 Ⓦ www.bishopleihtl.com.hk Ⓝ MTR: Tsuen Wan or Island line to Central, then take the Mid-Levels Escalator up to Robinson Road

BP International £–££ The BP stands for Baden-Powell – yes, he of the Scout Association (which owns BP International). What's offered are comfortable, clean rooms that are a little short on designer flair. A good place if you're travelling with kids, not least because Kowloon Park is extremely close. Ⓐ 8 Austin Road, Tsim Sha Tsui ☎ 2376 1111 Ⓦ www.bpih.com.hk Ⓝ MTR: Tsuen Wan line to Jordan

Eaton Hotel £–££ This has a great fourth-floor lobby lounge, a rooftop pool and comfortable guest rooms. Near Temple Street Night Market. Ⓐ 380 Nathan Road, Yau Ma Tei ☎ 2782 1818 Ⓦ www.hongkong.eatonhotels.com Ⓝ MTR: Tsuen Wan line to Jordan

Rosedale on the Park £–££ Right across from Victoria Park, this cyber-hotel has a boutique atmosphere with mod cons galore. Ⓐ 8 Shelter Street, Causeway Bay ☎ 2127 8888 Ⓦ www.rosedale.com.hk Ⓝ MTR: Island line to Causeway Bay

Langham Place ££ A modern, chic establishment in the heart of Mong Kok's traditional sights and sounds. Also conveniently attached to the glitzy Langham Place Mall and a subway station. Ⓐ 555 Shanghai Street, Mong Kok ☎ 3552 3388 Ⓦ hongkong.langhamplacehotels.com Ⓝ MTR: Tsuen Wan or Kwun Tong line to Mong Kok

Lan Kwai Fong Hotel ££ You can't get any closer to the action than with this boutique hotel. Rooms are modern with elegant Chinese touches. In addition to the usual amenities, the staff are happy to arrange local tours and visa applications. Ⓐ 3 Kau U Fong, Central

☎ 3650 0000 **Ⓦ** www.lankwaifonghotel.com.hk **Ⓜ** MTR: Tsuen Wan or Island line to Central

Metropark Hotel ££ Cheery, comfortable, contemporary, with free broadband Internet, a rooftop pool and great harbour views. **⊛** 148 Tung Lo Wan Road, Causeway Bay **☎** 2600 1000 **Ⓦ** www.metroparkhotel.com **Ⓜ** MTR: Island line to Causeway Bay

Grand Hyatt Hong Kong £££ Sumptuous and up-to-the-minute, this is Hyatt's flagship hotel in Asia. Every service imaginable, including the largest outdoor pool in the city and the much-praised Plateau Spa. **⊛** 1 Harbour Road, Wan Chai **☎** 2588 1234 **Ⓦ** www.hongkong.grand.hyatt.com **Ⓜ** MTR: Island line to Wan Chai

Kowloon Shangri-La £££ On the waterfront of Tsim Sha Tsui East, this hotel has spacious rooms, great views and all the amenities and services you'd expect from a Shangri-La establishment. **⊛** 64 Mody Road, Tsim Sha Tsui **☎** 2721 2111 **Ⓦ** www.shangri-la.com **Ⓜ** MTR: Tsuen Wan line to Tsim Sha Tsui

The Peninsula Hong Kong £££ The oldest, grandest, most famous hotel in Hong Kong, a stay here is a never-to-be-forgotten event. Prices are very high but you get a Rolls-Royce to take you shopping, spacious rooms, incomparable service, a practice music room and the grand Gaddi's Restaurant. **⊛** Salisbury Road, Tsim Sha Tsui **☎** 2920 2888 **Ⓦ** www.peninsula.com **Ⓜ** MTR: Tsuen Wan line to Tsim Sha Tsui

The Upper House £££ Revel in panoramic harbour and island views from this intimate boutique hotel set atop premier retail complex Pacific Place. With its understated residential calmness, The Upper

◆ The Peninsula offers luxury accommodation – at a price

House offers luxury on a more personal scale than anywhere else in Hong Kong. ➋ 88 Queensway, Pacific Place ➊ 2918 1838 ⓦ www.upperhouse.com Ⓝ MTR: Island line to Admiralty

HOSTELS

One option you should always consider is to check out the **Youth Hostels Association** (➊ 2788 1638 ⓦ www.yha.org.hk). Affiliated to the International Youth Hostel Federation, this non-profit organisation accredits and oversees several hostels across Hong Kong. Cooking, laundry and Internet facilities are standard.

Ascension House £ If you don't mind commuting by rail into the city, this hostel on a mountain in the jungle in the New Territories is one of the best deals you'll find. Clean dorm beds, three meals a day and laundry for good rates. ➋ 33 Tao Fong Shan Road, Sha Tin ➊ 2691 4196 Ⓝ MTR: East Rail line to Sha Tin

⬥ Take to the water for the best view of Hong Kong

Booth Lodge £ Run by the Salvation Army, Booth Lodge is clean, spartan and convenient for the Mass Transit Railway (MTR) and various markets. ⓐ 11 Wing Sing Lane, Yau Ma Tei ⓣ 2771 9266 ⓦ http://boothlodge.salvation.org.hk ⓝ MTR: Tsuen Wan or Kwun Tong line to Yau Ma Tei

Hong Kong Hostel £ Quiet and clean, this is one of the best deals on Hong Kong Island. Most rooms have phones, fridges and TV. There are cooking and laundry facilities plus a computer room. ⓐ Flat A2, 3rd Floor, Paterson Building, 47 Paterson Street, Causeway Bay ⓣ 2895 1015 ⓦ http://hostel.hk ⓝ MTR: Island line to Causeway Bay

Noble Hostel £ An immaculately clean, conveniently located guesthouse with a good reputation, so book ahead. All 45 rooms have a phone, fridge and air conditioning. ⓐ Flat A3, 7th Floor, Great George Building, 27 Paterson Street, Causeway Bay ⓣ 2576 6148 ⓦ www.noblehostel.com.hk ⓝ MTR: Island line to Causeway Bay

The Salisbury YMCA £ Excellent value and also terrific when travelling with kids. It's a two-minute walk to the Star Ferry and TST subway, and has suites for families, an inexpensive café, a kids' swimming pool, indoor climbing wall and much more. ⓐ Salisbury Road, Tsim Sha Tsui ⓣ 2268 7000 ⓦ www.ymcahk.org.hk ⓝ MTR: Tsuen Wan line to Tsim Sha Tsui

CAMPSITES

There are many holiday camps and campsites in the New Territories. Listings can be found through the **Leisure and Cultural Services Department** (ⓣ 2414 5555 ⓦ www.lcsd.gov.hk).

THE BEST OF HONG KONG

You'd be surprised at how much you can pack into a short time in Hong Kong – between the excellent public transport, late opening times and the fact that everything is so close by, you really have no excuse not to tick every one of these off.

TOP 10 ATTRACTIONS

- **Peak experience** Take the funicular tramway to the top of Victoria Peak for a view that will knock your socks off. Try it again at night (see pages 66–7).

- **Tailored to a T** Head to the tailor and get measured for the best-fitting outfit in your wardrobe. Don't expect it within a day, though (see page 24).

- **Walled city** The Sam Tung Uk Museum – a restored Hakka walled village – takes you on a time trip to view life in the 18th century (see page 99).

- **The Tian Tan Buddha** The world's largest seated outdoor bronze Buddha. Follow this with a vegetarian lunch at the Po Lin Monastery (see pages 110 & 111).

- **Fortune smiles** There's no better place than superstitious Hong Kong to have your Chinese horoscope prepared at the Temple Street Night Market (see page 82).

- **A change is as good as a rest** Take a breather from Hong Kong congestion to hike in the remote regions of the New Territories, taking in abandoned villages and rice fields, sweeping vistas, beaches and old Taoist shrines (see pages 94–104).

- **A stellar trip** As Hong Kong's quintessential mode of travel, the Star Ferry is a must for a cheap harbour tour and great skyline photos (see page 45).

- **Morning meditation** After a quick introduction to tai chi, join the skilled practitioners in one of the city's parks (see page 35).

- **Party central** Rest up in the day, then dance until dawn in the discos and clubs of swinging Lan Kwai Fong (see page 30).

- **Cheap sightseeing** Ride the double-decker tram from one side of Hong Kong Island to the other (see page 44).

◆ *The Hong Kong Convention & Exhibition Centre*

Suggested itineraries

HALF-DAY: HONG KONG IN A HURRY

For a quick taster, stick to Central. Follow the signs to the Peak tram station on Garden Road and hop on board to Victoria Peak (see pages 66–7). Back down in Central, take the double-decker tram for a mini-tour of the island or try a walking tour. Finally, head for Pacific Place (see page 70) to splurge on designer threads or window-shop.

⬥ The Flagstaff House Museum of Tea Ware

1 DAY: TIME TO SEE A LITTLE MORE

Start with a *dim sum* breakfast at City Hall Maxim's Palace (see page 29), then head for Victoria Peak. Back at sea level, check out the tea ceremony at the Flagstaff House Museum of Tea Ware (see page 67) before taking the **Star Ferry** (ⓦ www.starferry.com.hk) for a harbour experience to Kowloon. Lovers of gemstones should visit Yau Ma Tei's Jade Market (see page 78). If you prefer clothes shopping, try Mong Kok's Ladies' Market (see page 80). After a drink at the Peninsula's Felix (see page 93), have dinner in Kowloon and end the day back on the harbourfront watching the Symphony of Lights laser show (see page 83).

2–3 DAYS: TIME TO SEE MUCH MORE

Visit the New Territories to see the Hong Kong Heritage Museum (see page 96) and the Sam Tung Uk Museum (see page 99). Hike along the Lung Yeuk Tau Heritage Trail to see some fascinating historical buildings and a glimpse of life hundreds of years ago. The Mai Po Wetlands (see page 98), with more than 300 bird species, including black-faced spoonbills, is an alternative. Explore some of the Outer Islands like Lamma (see pages 118–21) to hike, swim or dine alfresco on the waterfront. On Lantau Island (see page 108), climb up to the world's largest seated bronze Buddha, or take the Ngong Ping Cable Car. If you have kids in tow, take them to Hong Kong Disneyland® (see pages 108 & 110).

LONGER: ENJOYING HONG KONG TO THE FULL

Take a trip to Macau (see pages 122–34) to see the Las Vegas of the East, and the remaining mesh of Chinese and Portuguese cultures; or visit bordering cities like Shenzhen (see pages 135–42) and Guangzhou in mainland China.

Something for nothing

Some of the best things in Hong Kong life are free – including panoramic views of the city you catch from the public viewing gallery on the 43rd floor of the Bank of China Tower in Central (see page 64). There are great views, too, on several hikes in the New Territories, including the MacLehose and Wilson trails. The Mid-Levels Escalator (the world's longest) is another freebie, although it may amuse kids more than adults.

On Lantau Island (see pages 108–14), there are walking trails galore, and for the grand finale a 260-step climb to yet another superlative – the Tian Tan Buddha (see pages 111–12).

Hong Kong has a 'Meet the People' programme (contact the HKTB, see page 152, for details), where you can learn tai chi, and find out about pearls, jade, Chinese antiques and more – for free. Take a walk around the **Ng Tung Chai Waterfall** and streams just north of Tai Mo Shan, Hong Kong's tallest mountain. Southwest of the village of Ng Tung Chai, the **Kadoorie Farm & Botanic Garden** (ⓦ www.kfbg.org.hk) is a conservation and teaching centre with lovely gardens, made even lovelier as they're free to peruse.

The Zoological & Botanic Gardens (see page 67) is a collection of sculptures, fountains, greenhouses, a zoo and a wonderful aviary – all to be savoured at no cost. The Yuen Po Street Bird Garden (see page 83) is set inside a Chinese courtyard filled with a multitude of birds and cages for sale, though a quick shufti won't cost a penny. Like many other places, Hong Kong has a day (Wednesdays) when admission is free at most museums.

The waterfront Tsim Sha Tsui East Promenade is a great place to jog or stroll during the day and an eye-popping vista on to illuminated Central at night. You can't whack a bit of *flânerie*, and the HKTB has free booklets (with maps) called 'Hong Kong Walks' and 'Hong Kong Unique Tours and Hiking Tours'. For film buffs, the promenade has an Avenue of the Stars that pays homage to the local film industry and its stars. You can also watch the Symphony of Lights here – a spectacular sound-and-light show utilising several buildings in Hong Kong's skyline (see page 83). Dramatic lights dance and flash nightly for around 20 minutes from 20.00.

● *The city shows off every night, with the Symphony of Lights*

When it rains

In this humid subtropical climate, don't be surprised if you hit a shower or two. In spring and late summer, the rain can be torrential, providing a good excuse for indoor activities – starting with a *dim sum* breakfast in one of the city's livelier spots. Then enjoy the huge variety of museums: wine or racing museum, museum of history, even a pawn shop museum in Macau. The Hong Kong Heritage Museum (see page 96) is a must, where, in addition to all the treasures, you can visit the **Cantonese Opera Heritage Hall** (☎ 2180 8188), watch old operas on video with English subtitles and virtually make yourself up as a Cantonese opera character on a computer. There's also a **Police Museum** (free) in Wan Chai Gap (☎ 27 Coombe Road ☎ 2849 7019) that tells the history of the Hong Kong police force, narcotics and triads.

No one knows tea quite like the Chinese, but you can catch a glimmer in a Chinese Tea Appreciation class (free) – like the one run by Mr Ip Wing-chi at the **Lock Cha Tea Shop** (☎ Ground Floor, The K S Lo Gallery, Hong Kong Park ☎ 2801 7177 ⓦ www.lockcha.com) every Monday and Thursday – and learn all about the varieties, proper preparation techniques and tea-drinking etiquette. Next door in the Flagstaff House Museum of Tea Ware (see page 67) is a mini-museum with a collection of rare teapots.

If Hong Kong is anything, it's shopping-centre heaven. For upmarket shops, Central has the swanky **ifc mall** (ⓦ www.ifc.com.hk) and Pacific Place (see page 70), while Times Square and Jardine's Crescent have lower-priced clothing. On the Kowloon side, head to Elements Mall (see page 86) or the **Langham Place Mall** (ⓦ www.langhamplace.com.hk). Not so well known are the micro malls crammed into old buildings or above MTR stations where you can find designer clothes, funky footwear and kooky accessories.

Best times to shop are between 15.00 and 22.00 at places like the **Up Date Mall** in Tsim Sha Tsui (ⓐ 36–44 Nathan Road), the **Trendy Zone** in Mong Kok (ⓐ 580 Nathan Road) and the **Beverley Commercial Centre** in Tsim Sha Tsui (ⓐ 87–105 Chatham Road South). For furniture and home accessories, hop into a cab and head to **Horizon Plaza** in Ap Lei Chau (ⓐ 2 Lee Wing Street) on the south side of Hong Kong Island, where numerous stores sell modern and reasonably priced pieces.

At the day's end, mosey down to SoHo or LKF for happy-hour drinks that will probably stretch on ... it's a great way to meet locals and wait for the showers to end.

◔ *There are tea appreciation classes for serious tea drinkers*

On arrival

TIME DIFFERENCE

Hong Kong is eight hours ahead of GMT and does not have daylight saving.

ARRIVING

By air

Hong Kong International Airport (☎ 2181 0000 ⓦ www.hongkong airport.com) was considered the world's largest civil engineering project when it opened in mid-1998, and its two terminals are some of the world's busiest. It sits on Chek Lap Kok, a small island off the northern coast of Lantau, and is connected to the mainland by several spans, including Tsing Ma Bridge, one of the world's largest suspension bridges. The airport is about 32 km (20 miles) from Hong Kong's central business district. Its two runways operate 24 hours a day and the baggage-handling system delivers bags in approximately ten minutes.

With its modern and user-friendly design, the airport combines a pleasant ambience with a tranquil green environment plus excellent facilities and services – the usual cafeterias and restaurants, lounges, a beauty salon, shower rooms, foot massage, pharmacy and business centre. Banks and ATMs are available in the arrivals and departures halls.

The dedicated Airport Express runs from 05.50 to 00.45 daily, with trains coming at 12-minute intervals. It takes about 25 minutes to get into Central and is by far the most convenient way to get into town. A return ticket to Hong Kong Island costs HK$180 and discounts are available for groups of two or more. There is also free in-town check-in and a shuttle bus service available in Hong Kong and Kowloon for Airport Express passengers, as well as free porter services at all the Airport Express stations.

For the more budget-conscious, **Cityflyer Airbuses** (☎ 2873 0818 🌐 www.nwstbus.com.hk) has ticket counters in the airport arrivals hall with buses departing every 10 to 30 minutes. Round-trip fares cost between HK$55 and HK$65 depending on where you go; the exact fare is required.

For details on operating times for buses and trains, visit 🌐 www.hongkongairport.com and click on 'Transport'.

The **Airport Shuttle** (☎ 2735 7823) provides door-to-door service between the airport and major hotels. Tickets are available through your hotel or at a counter in the arrivals hall, and cost depends on your destination. It takes about 30 to 40 minutes to reach Kowloon and 60 minutes to Hong Kong Island.

🔺 *Hong Kong International Airport's 1.3-km (3/4-mile)-long passenger terminal*

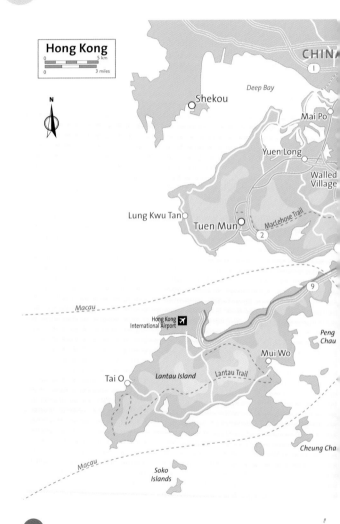

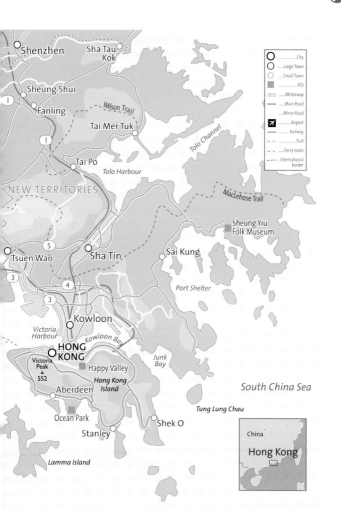

Taxis are always available and are relatively inexpensive. They take about 30–45 minutes to Kowloon and 60 minutes to Hong Kong Island. They cost from HK$300 up, depending on destination.

By rail

Unless you're coming from the west via China, it's unlikely you'd arrive in Hong Kong by train. That said, the **Hong Kong MTR** (☎ 2881 8888 ⓦ www.mtr.com.hk) provides intercity rail services from Guangdong, Beijing and Shanghai. The Guangdong Through Train takes under 2 hours and runs 12 times daily. The Beijing–Kowloon Through Train, which takes about 24 hours, and the 19-hour Shanghai–Kowloon Through Train operate on alternate days. The MTR website provides ticket and schedule information.

By road

Again, there are no highway links except from mainland China. Citybus routes link the Shenzhen economic zone and Hong Kong, and there's a coach service from Guangzhou.

By water

It's also unlikely you will arrive by sea, unless it's with one of about 30 international cruise ships that dock at the Ocean Terminal in Tsim Sha Tsui. However, you can arrive from Macau by ferry (see pages 122 & 124).

FINDING YOUR FEET

The biggest problem a visitor may have to deal with when visiting Hong Kong is the weather – particularly in the summer when it's stiflingly humid. Dress lightly but always carry something to throw over your shoulders when you go into a restaurant, since the air conditioning may be more suitable for penguins than people.

Despite its size and frenzied intensity, Hong Kong is a safe city and visitors feel secure walking almost anywhere, even at night – although it's best to use common sense and stick to well-lit areas. In most of the heavily touristy areas like Tsim Sha Tsui and Wan Chai, police patrol to watch out for pickpockets who work in gangs. It's always a good idea to keep your valuables in the hotel safe along with your passport, and carry with you only what you need.

ORIENTATION

People not familiar with Asia might think Hong Kong is just one island or one city, but it's actually divided into four distinct parts: Hong Kong Island, Kowloon Peninsula, the New Territories and the outlying islands. The whole area is known as the SAR (Special Administrative Region) and much of it is mountainous.

Both Hong Kong Island and Kowloon are further subdivided into districts, with Central being the prime business and financial district on Hong Kong Island. The others are Causeway Bay, Western and Wan Chai (see page 62).

In Kowloon (see pages 78–93), tourists are usually most familiar with Tsim Sha Tsui (where most of the hotels, museums and shops are) along with Tsim Sha Tsui East, Mong Kok and Yau Ma Tei. West Kowloon has in the last few years become the top choice of multinationals relocating from Central to avoid high rentals. Since these areas are so compact, Hong Kong is easy to navigate.

The largest area in the SAR is taken up by the New Territories (see pages 94–104), which start at the northern edge of Kowloon and stretch all the way to the Chinese border. Back in the 1960s, this was a highly rural area made up of vast green stretches dotted with small villages and farms, and even though much still remains uninhabited, the Territories have changed enormously. Huge public-

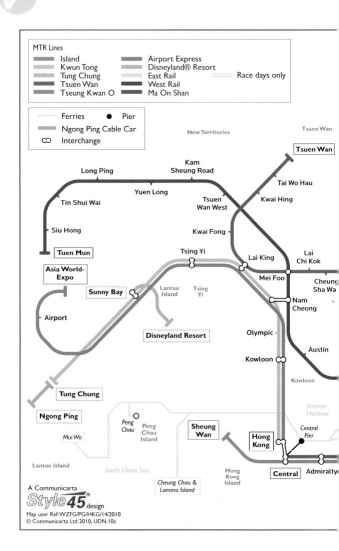

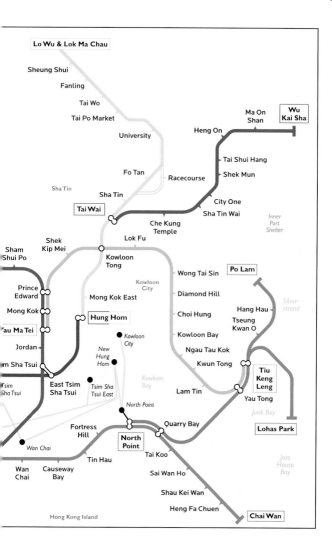

housing projects have pushed the population up to almost half the total number of people in Hong Kong.

While visitors usually only get to four or five of the outlying islands, there are actually 260 in all, most of them barren and uninhabited. Cheung Chau (see pages 114–18), Lantau (see pages 108–14) and Lamma (see pages 118–21) are the most popular and accessible.

GETTING AROUND

Hong Kong is definitely a city for walkers (though public transport can make exploration of the New Territories considerably easier; see page 94). Get a good street map (available free from HKTB or your hotel) and find the main thoroughfares and streets. On Hong Kong Island, Des Voeux Road Central, Queen's Road Central and Connaught Road are the main roads with Hennessy Road and Gloucester Road leading east through Wan Chai to Causeway Bay. On the Kowloon side, Nathan Road stretching north is the most important artery, with Salisbury Road running east and west from the Star Ferry through Tsim Sha Tsui. There's also a promenade along the waterfront.

Public transport is safe, inexpensive and highly reliable and will let you get to almost anywhere you want to go within an hour. Just be sure to avoid rush hours (08.00–10.00 and 17.00–19.00). Buses require exact change, so check the fare before you board.

The cleanest, fastest and most efficient way to get around is via the Mass Transit Railway (MTR). This system is always on time. The network is made up of interconnected lines, which are colour coded for ease (see map, pages 56–7). Trains run every two to ten minutes from around 06.00 to approximately 01.00. The MTR is fully automated. Just hold your Octopus Card (see page 60) to the scanner

◆ Jump on one of the classic Hong Kong trams

OCTOPUS CARD

For more than a one- or two-day stay, use an Octopus Card for getting around. This is valid on most forms of transport and will even allow you to make small purchases at some retail outlets such as 7-Eleven. You can buy Octopus Cards at ticket offices or customer services centres in any MTR station.

Octopus Cards ☎ 2266 2222 ⓦ www.octopus.com.hk

at the turnstile, which will automatically deduct the fare. For short trips between Hong Kong and Kowloon, use the Star Ferry at a quarter the cost.

Taxis are also cheap and plentiful, although you might get stuck in bumper-to-bumper traffic during rush hours.

CAR HIRE

Because Hong Kong public transport is so good and traffic so frenzied, most people opt not to hire a car. For trips to the New Territories, there are a number of companies that will rent on a daily, weekend or weekly rate (visit Hong Kong Yellow Pages at ⓦ www.yp.com.hk). Most firms accept International Driving Permits or driving licences from your home country. Drivers must be at least 25 years of age. For a car with a driver, check **Ace Hire Car Service** (☎ 2572 7663 ⓦ www.acehirecar.com.hk).

▶ *Travel by tram up to Victoria Peak*

THE CITY OF
Hong Kong

Hong Kong Island

Looking at images of Hong Kong, the first impression is that of a dense forest of skyscrapers and nothing more. But this is far from the reality. Hong Kong is actually a collection of neighbourhoods, each with a special character.

Central, in the very north of Hong Kong Island, is where the colony began in 1842. Today, it is the seat of government and the city's most important financial district.

Within Central are smaller neighbourhoods such as Lan Kwai Fong (LKF), a popular entertainment area playing host to a range of restaurants and bars frequented mostly by people in their 20s and 30s out to have a good – and loud – time.

SoHo (South of Hollywood Road) is also a dining-and-nightlife district but a little trendier and more sane than LKF, popular with an older and more moneyed crowd.

Hovering over Central, Victoria Peak is the island's most famous mountain and most exclusive address.

To the east of Central, Wan Chai and Causeway Bay are where you find the best in shopping and nightlife. To the northwest is Sheung Wan – an older, more distinctly Chinese neighbourhood with antiques, funeral shops, Chinese medicine and those omnipresent 'chop' makers.

Aberdeen, on the south side of Hong Kong Island, was once a fishing village but is now a forest of high-rises and housing projects. It's also where you can still find sampans and Jumbo Kingdom, the famous floating restaurant (see page 66), as well as Ocean Park (see page 66), with its aquarium and amusement rides.

Stanley, on the quiet south side of the islands, was also a fishing village but is now the best discount marketplace for anything from shoes to souvenirs and silk suits.

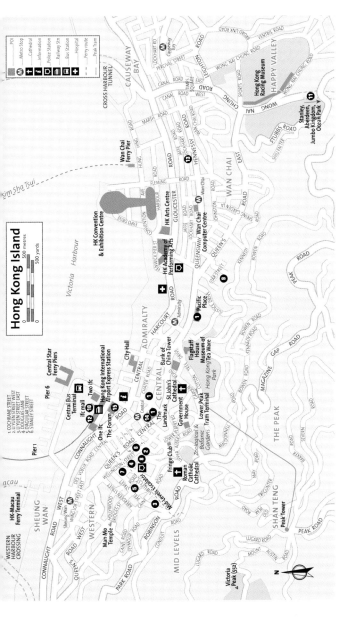

SIGHTS & ATTRACTIONS

Bank of China Tower

This building is worth seeing, not least because it's the best-known modern architectural symbol on the island and was designed by renowned architect I M Pei. What makes a visit to it even more worthwhile is knowing a little about the controversy it has stirred up since its conception. Hong Kong is obsessed by feng shui and the 70-storey building's sharp angles were rumoured to be a symbolic dagger directing hostility towards Government House. The two antennae on top of the building were said to resemble incense burnt for the dead. All this was also said to have affected the excellent feng shui of the HSBC Building – at least until Lee Ka-shing built the Cheung Kong Center between them and restored much of the harmony and energy flow. There is a viewing gallery on the 43rd floor that's open during business hours and free to visit.
ⓐ 1 Garden Road, Central ⓣ 2332 3328 ⓛ 09.00–16.30 Mon–Fri, 09.00–12.30 Sat, closed Sun Ⓜ MTR: Tsuen Wan or Island line to Central

Golden Bauhinia Square

The 6-m (19-ft)-tall Forever Blooming Bauhinia, a gift from the people of China to Hong Kong to mark the handover in 1997, stands on the edge of the Hong Kong Convention & Exhibition Centre. Every morning at 07.50 – weather permitting – you can catch the pomp and circumstance of the flag-raising ceremony. On the first day of each month, the five uniformed officers are joined by a rifle escort team in full ceremonial dress, a police band and a pipe band. ⓐ Wan Chai waterfront ⓣ 2814 4279 ⓛ 24 hours Ⓜ MTR: Island line to Wan Chai

◆ Bank of China Tower

Jumbo Kingdom

Located in Aberdeen, this area is famous for its reinvented 'kingdom' – home to a colourful floating seafood restaurant-cum-shopping venue, and a flotilla of junks interspersed with fishing boats and yachts. This is the place to hire a sampan (usually manned by a woman!) for a tour around the harbour to glimpse what life is like living on a junk. ❷ Aberdeen Harbour ❶ 2553 9111 Ⓦ www.jumbo.com.hk 🕒 11.00–23.30 Mon–Sat, 07.30–23.30 Sun Ⓝ Bus: 75 from Exchange Square (near Central MTR station) to Shum Wan Pier

Ocean Park

Close to Jumbo Kingdom is this combined amusement and marine park. It has a first-class aquarium and zoo where you can see pandas, walk the dinosaur trail and wander through a magical butterfly house. Well worth an afternoon visit. ❷ Ocean Park, Aberdeen ❶ 2552 0291 Ⓦ www.oceanpark.com.hk 🕒 10.00–18.00 Ⓝ Bus: 629 from Admiralty MTR station or from Central Pier 7

Victoria Peak

This is Hong Kong Island's highest peak. Naturally, that makes it the best place to take those classic shots of the city – especially if it is a clear day. A century ago, getting to the top of the peak meant a three-hour trip in sedan chairs for the rich who lived there. Today, the Peak Tram runs every ten to fifteen minutes for the eight-minute trip. At the top, there's **Madame Tussauds** wax museum (Ⓦ www.madame-tussauds.com.hk), **EA Experience** for gaming enthusiasts (Ⓦ www.eaexperience.com), plus the Sky Terrace, a 360-degree viewing platform on the fourth floor of the Peak Tower. If you don't fancy being cooped up in the shopping complex, take a circular hike through banyan trees and lush vegetation on the Peak Trail. ⓦ www.thepeak.com.hk ⓛ The Peak Tram runs daily from 07.00 to 24.00

Zoological & Botanic Gardens

Come in the early morning and you can either observe or take part in calming, meditative tai chi exercises. Quiet pathways lined with semitropical trees and flowers lead to a small zoo with various mammals and reptiles, and an aviary with more than 300 species of birds. ⓐ Upper Albert Road (opposite Government House; enter on Garden Road) ⓣ 2530 0155 ⓦ www.lcsd.gov.hk ⓛ 06.00–19.00 ⓜ MTR: Tsuen Wan or Island line to Central

CULTURE

Flagstaff House Museum of Tea Ware

Whether tea intrigues you or not, the tea ceremony is an integral part of Chinese culture. This museum (which is in Hong Kong Park) is the oldest colonial building in Hong Kong and is the best place to see mid-19th-century architecture. You can marvel at some of the 600-piece collection of tea ware or buy replicas in the gift shop. ⓐ 10 Cotton Tree Drive ⓣ 2869 0690 ⓦ www.lcsd.gov.hk ⓛ 10.00–17.00 Wed–Mon, closed Tues ⓜ MTR: Island line to Admiralty

Man Mo Temple

This is one of the oldest and most famous temples in Hong Kong and is named after two deities: one (Man Tai), the god of literature, and the other (Mo Tai), the god of war. The whole place has a mysterious atmosphere, with giant incense cones suspended from the ceiling, worshippers lighting more cones and fortune-tellers waiting to advise you of your fate. ⓐ 124–126 Hollywood Road

☎ 2540 0350 ⏰ 08.00–18.00 Ⓜ MTR: Tsuen Wan or Island line
to Central

RETAIL THERAPY

If you are coming to Hong Kong to shop, then do beware of falling
prey to opportunists intent on obtaining your money under false
pretences. Check that the shop or service provider displays a QTS
(Quality Tourism Service) sticker, which identifies shops and restaurants
that provide good service. The aim of the QTS Scheme, an initiative
of the Hong Kong Tourism Board, is to give consumers protection.
A list of QTS-accredited establishments is available from HKTB
(see page 152).

LABELS TO LOOK FOR

For designs with a difference – and a refreshing change
from the usual high-street collections – check out these
local designers who are really making waves (and clothes):
Lulu Cheung (Ⓦ www.lulucheung.com.hk) specialises in
contemporary womenswear. With his pricey couture creations,
Barney Cheng (Ⓦ www.barneycheng.com) is famed for being
the designer to the stars. **Ruby Li** (Ⓦ www.rubyli.com.hk) creates
designs with young street attitude, plus a funky range of jewellery
and handbags. **Dorian Ho** (Ⓦ www.dorianho.net) mixes
de-luxe fabrics with contemporary designs and also has a
bridal collection. Internationally renowned designer **Vivienne
Tam**'s (Ⓦ www.viviennetam.com) signature style is in modern,
wearable apparel with elegant ethnic touches.

◆ *Shop in comfort in pristine Pacific Place*

Hollywood Road Most of Hong Kong's reputable antique shops are here. You can find luxury ticket items such as Ming dynasty vases, furniture and jewellery. MTR: Tsuen Wan or Island line to Central

The Lanes This is shopping as old as Hong Kong itself. Here stalls sell just about everything from watches and toys to clothes and souvenirs. Keep an eye out for the shops on either side tucked away in basements or up some narrow stairs, where some of the best bargains are to be had. Three narrow alleyways in Central – Douglas Lane, Li Yuen Street East and Li Yuen Street West – which run parallel to each other between Des Voeux and Queen's roads 10.00–21.00 MTR: Tsuen Wan or Island line to Central

Pacific Place For those who like their shopping sleek, chic and well designed. You'll find popular department stores like Lane Crawford and Seibu, as well as smart clothing boutiques, restaurants, hotels and a cinema. 88 Queensway, Central 2844 8988 www.pacificplace.com.hk 10.00–20.30 MTR: Island line to Admiralty

Wan Chai Computer Centre Two floors of small shops packed with computers, consumer electronics, accessories and everything else a gadget junkie needs. Remember to compare prices and haggle. 130 Hennessy Road, Wan Chai 12.00–21.00 MTR: Island line to Wan Chai

TAKING A BREAK

Cova £ With its yummy Italian pastries, good coffee and fantastic gelati, this is a chain to look out for. Branches on Hong Kong Island

include Pacific Place, The Landmark and Prince's Building. ☎ 2832 9008
🌐 www.cova.com.hk 🕑 12.00–22.00

Good Luck Thai Café £ ❷ A highly popular place tucked down a side
street in LKF known colloquially as Rat Alley. But don't let that put
you off; it's clean and the food is low-cost and tasty. 🏠 13 Wing Wah
Lane, Lan Kwai Fong ☎ 2877 2971 🕑 12.00–24.00 Ⓜ MTR: Tsuen Wan
or Island line to Central; walk up D'Aguilar Street and take the first
right turn after Wellington Street

Life Organic Health Cafe £ ❸ Wholesome vegetarian food so
delicious that it's guaranteed to appeal even to carnivores. The rooftop
terrace is great for an alfresco break. 🏠 10 Shelley Street, Central
☎ 2810 9777 🌐 www.lifecafe.com.hk 🕑 12.00–15.00, 18.00–22.00
Ⓜ MTR: Tsuen Wan or Island line to Central

Tsim Chai Kee Noodle £ ❹ Some of the best prawn dumpling
noodles in town, dished up at rapid-fire speed. 🏠 98 Wellington
Street, Central ☎ 2850 6471 🕑 11.30–21.30 Ⓜ MTR: Tsuen Wan or
Island line to Central

Chocolux Cafe ££ ❺ As the name suggests, the cocoa bean in every
mouthwatering shape and indulgent form – cakes, crêpes and even
cocktails. Tucked away on Peel Street in SoHo. 🏠 57 Peel Street,
Central ☎ 2858 6760 🌐 www.chocoluxcafe.com 🕑 12.00–24.00
Sun–Thur, 12.00–01.00 Fri & Sat Ⓜ MTR: Tsuen Wan or Island line
to Central

Luk Yu Tea House ££ ❻ This Art Deco Cantonese restaurant is the
most famous tea house in Hong Kong, complete with period spittoons.

You can try a whole range of teas here from jasmine flavoured to daffodil, but the place is even more famous for its *dim sum*, which is served 07.00–17.30. ❷ 24–26 Stanley Street, Central ❶ 2523 5464 ❷ 07.00–22.00 Ⓜ MTR: Tsuen Wan or Island line to Central

AFTER DARK

RESTAURANTS

Flower Trump Restaurant £ ❼ An excellent place to sample some Shanghai-style cuisine. Start with some steamed dumplings before moving on to the minced pork with sesame seed buns and the braised spicy bean curd. ❷ G/F, 18–20 Lyndhurst Terrace, off Peel Street, Central ❶ 2126 7266 Ⓦ www.flower-trump.com ❷ 11.00–21.30 Ⓜ MTR: Tsuen Wan or Island line to Central

Tapeo £–££ ❽ An authentic Spanish tapas bar serving a wide range of tapas and wines in an open-kitchen-style environment. Located at the bustling and newly fashionable crossroads of LKF and SoHo, where Hollywood Road and Wyndham Street merge. ❷ G/F Au's Building, 19 Hollywood Road, Central ❶ 3171 1989 Ⓦ www.tapeo.hk ❷ 12.00–15.00, 18.00–23.00 daily Ⓜ MTR: Tsuen Wan or Island line to Central

Chez Patrick ££ ❾ With an ever-changing dinner menu depending on what's in season, this cosy French fine-dining restaurant is a little gem in the heart of Wan Chai. ❷ 8–9 Sun Street, Wan Chai ❶ 2527 1408 Ⓦ www.chezpatrick.hk ❷ 12.00–15.00, 19.00–23.00 Mon–Sat, closed Sun Ⓜ MTR. Island line to Admiralty

Isola Bar + Grill ££ ❿ Thin-crust pizza and home-made pastas, sauced and cooked to perfection, Isola serves up simple rustic Italian

cuisine in über-slick minimalist interiors. The winning combination of impeccable service, an alfresco terrace and stunning harbour views makes this one of the most popular spots in town.
Ⓐ 3/F, ifc mall, 8 Finance Street, Central Ⓣ 2383 8765
Ⓦ www.isolabarandgrill.com Ⓛ 12.00–14.30, 18.30–23.00 Sun–Thur, 18.30–23.30 Fri & Sat Ⓝ MTR: Tsuen Wan or Island line to Central, or Tung Chung line to Hong Kong

Lucy's ££ ⑪ After a hard day haggling in Stanley Market, Lucy's is a small, cosy spot just off the main drag where you can choose from a short menu that offers the freshest choices in season. The daily special is a good bet. Ⓐ 64 Stanley Main Street, Stanley Ⓣ 2813 9055 Ⓛ 12.00–15.00, 19.00–22.00 Mon–Fri, 12.00–16.00, 18.30–22.00 Sat & Sun Ⓝ Bus: 6, 6A or 6X from Central

Sen-ryo ££ ⑫ A sushi bar that's ideal for a light and quiet dinner with cool, pared-down décor to match. Choose between conveyor-belt seating and a more intimate booth. The soft-shell crab handrolls are a must-try. Ⓐ Level 3, Shop 3099–3100, ifc mall, Central Ⓣ 2234 7633 Ⓛ 11.30–23.00 Ⓝ MTR: Tung Chung line to Hong Kong

Amuse Bouche £££ ⑬ Fabulous French food, designer interiors and spectacular city views make this fine-dining restaurant a gem. The well-considered menu shows individual flair with carefully crafted and presented dishes, and one of the best wine lists in Hong Kong, not only by stock, but also by price. Ⓐ 22/F, The Hennessy, 256 Hennessy Road, Wan Chai Ⓣ 2891 3666 Ⓦ www.amusebouche.com.hk Ⓛ 12.00–14.30, 18.30–24.00 Mon–Fri, 18.30–24.00 Sat & Sun Ⓝ MTR: Island line to Wan Chai

L'Atelier de Joel Robuchon £££ The stylish and slick Hong Kong outpost of Michelin-star chef Joel Robuchon's diner-style restaurant, serving creative tasting menus. ❸ Shop 401, 4/F, The Landmark, Central ❶ 2166 9000 Ⓦ www.joel-robuchon.com Ⓛ 12.00–14.30, 18.30–22.30 Ⓝ MTR: Tsuen Wan or Island line to Central

Hunan Garden £££ Enjoy spicy Hunan cuisine and a great view of the harbour. ❸ The Forum, 3rd Floor, Exchange Square, Central ❶ 2868 2880 Ⓛ 11.00–15.00, 17.30–23.30 Ⓝ MTR: Tsuen Wan or Island line to Central

BARS, CLUBS & LIVE PERFORMANCE VENUES

Aqua Luna An old-world Chinese junk that crosses Victoria Harbour several times a day. Reservations necessary. ❶ 2116 8821 Ⓦ www.aqualuna.com.hk Ⓛ 13.30–14.45, 17.30–22.45 Ⓝ MTR: Tsuen Wan or Island line to Central or Tsuen Wan line to Tsim Sha Tsui

Divino If you don't feel like dressing up, come here for a relaxed cocktail and the happy-hour bar snack buffet. ❸ 73 Wyndham Street, Central ❶ 2167 8883 Ⓦ www.divino.com.hk Ⓛ 12.00–late Mon–Sat, 18.00–late Sun Ⓝ MTR: Tsuen Wan or Island line to Central

Dragon-i Firmly established as the place for the über-cool to party, the dancing goes on into the wee hours. ❸ 60 Wyndham Street, Central ❶ 3110 1222 Ⓦ www.dragon-i.com.hk Ⓛ 18.00–03.00 Mon–Sat, closed Sun Ⓝ MTR: Tsuen Wan or Island line to Central

Dusk Till Dawn If live cover bands belting out cheesy chart-toppers are your thing, look no further. The crowd is friendly, the drinks cheap and food and snacks served till 05.00. ❸ 76–84 Jaffe Road, Wan Chai

◯ Street cafés offer plenty of local flavour

☎ 2528 4689 🕐 12.00–06.00 Mon–Fri, 15.00–06.00 Sat & Sun
Ⓝ MTR: Island line to Wan Chai

The Fringe Club Here you'll find avant-garde performances by home-grown talent. It's best to check out the listings – everything from chanteuses to rock bands to jazz can be playing. ⓐ 2 Lower Albert Road, Central ☎ 2521 7251 ⓦ www.hkfringeclub.com Ⓝ MTR: Tsuen Wan or Island line to Central

The Globe The closest thing to an English pub that you'll find in these parts, The Globe boasts an impressive beer selection. ⓐ Garley Building, 45–53 Graham Street, Central ☎ 2543 1941 ⓦ www.theglobe.com.hk 🕐 10.00–late Mon–Fri Ⓝ MTR: Tsuen Wan or Island line to Central

Hong Kong Academy of Performing Arts Both student and professional companies stage their work at this venue, as well as local and visiting companies. Check out the free happy-hour performances and lunchtime concerts. ⓐ 1 Gloucester Road, Wan Chai ☎ 2584 8500 ⓦ www.hkapa.edu Ⓝ MTR: Island line to Admiralty

Hong Kong Convention & Exhibition Centre The venue for pop and rock concerts. Check its website for up-and-coming events. Alternatively, contact the centre direct. ⓐ 1 Harbour Road, Wan Chai ☎ 2582 8888 ⓦ www.hkcec.com.hk Ⓝ MTR: Island line to Wan Chai

Lei Dou This bar has a Prohibition-era vibe that's a welcome relief from the frenzy of activity in the rest of the Fong, plus great Italian mojitos. ⓐ 1/F, 20–22 Lan Kwai Fong, Central ☎ 2525 6628 🕐 17.30–late Ⓝ MTR: Tsuen Wan or Island line to Central

The Pawn Housed in a heritage building, painstakingly restored, this was formerly used as a pawn shop. Serves modern British cuisine and great lagers on tap and has views over Hong Kong.
ⓐ 62 Johnston Road, Wan Chai ☎ 2866 3444
ⓦ www.thepawn.com.hk 🕑 11.00–15.00, 18.00–late daily
Ⓜ MTR: Island line to Wan Chai

Sugar Revel in the dazzling harbour views from the rooftop while the cocktails flow and the DJs spin their tunes. ⓐ 32/F, EAST Hotel, 29 Tai Koo Shing Road, Tai Koo Shing ☎ 3968 3738 ⓦ www.sugar-hongkong.com 🕑 17.00– 02.00 Mon–Sat, 13.00–23.00 Sun
Ⓜ MTR: Island line to Tai Koo

Takeout Comedy Club Hong Kong's first and only full-time comedy club features a varied programme of Chinese and English stand-up and improv comedy acts. Check the website for current acts and upcoming shows, or turn up and try your hand at their weekly open-mic nights every Tuesday. ⓐ 34 Elgin Street, SoHo ☎ 6220 4436
ⓦ www.takeoutcomedy.com 🕑 Vary; phone or see website
Ⓜ MTR: Tsuen Wan or Island line to Central

Tazmania Ballroom It's billiards meets ballroom and games meets glam at this gentlemen's-club-styled venue. There's a resident DJ mixing some of the best sounds in the city, an outdoor terrace, and a pool-playing area where the gold-plated pool tables rise up to reveal a dance floor. Guests are admitted at the discretion of the management, so dress the part. ⓐ 1/F, Lan Kwai Fong Tower, 33 Wyndham Street, Central ☎ 2801 5009 🕑 17.00–late daily
Ⓜ MTR: Tsuen Wan or Island line to Central

Kowloon

Kowloon lies just north of Hong Kong Island, a Star Ferry ride across Victoria Harbour. Its hills create a dramatic backdrop for what has been called 'one of the world's best cityscapes'. Kowloon actually means 'nine dragons', referring to the eight hills that represented the eight resident dragons; the ninth dragon was the emperor.

The northern border of Kowloon is Boundary Street and this separates the district from the New Territories. The main Kowloon districts are Tsim Sha Tsui, Tsim Sha Tsui East, Yau Ma Tei and Mong Kok. Despite its tongue-in-cheek nickname 'The Dark Side' – used mainly by Hong Kong Island residents too lazy to cross the harbour – Kowloon has emerged as an exciting shopping and entertainment district in its own right, shot through with streaks of charming local flavour.

Tourists are usually most familiar with Tsim Sha Tsui because this is where you'll find the greatest concentration of hotels, restaurants and shops as well as such attractions as the Hong Kong Space Museum (see pages 85–6), Kowloon Park (see page 80), a fine art museum and a cultural centre. The area also has a lively nightlife and what's known as 'the golden mile of shopping'.

Tsim Sha Tsui East is built on reclaimed land dotted with shopping, entertainment and restaurant complexes, hotels and some good museums.

Yau Ma Tei has a very 'Chinese' feel about it and some interesting markets – including the Jade Market and the Temple Street Night Market (see page 82). A good area to look for lower-priced hotels.

In addition to the swanky shopping mall/hotel complex Langham Place, Mong Kok is where you'll find the Yuen Po Street Bird Garden (see page 83), along with the Ladies' Market (see page 80) and a host of street stalls and food booths.

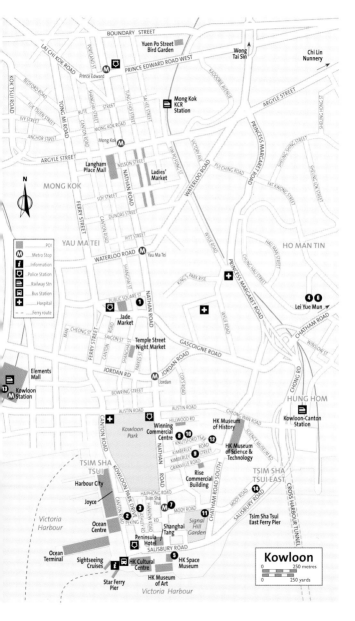

SIGHTS & ATTRACTIONS

Chi Lin Nunnery

A sprawling group of handcrafted timber buildings reconstructed in the classical Tang dynasty style, in particular wooden roofs erected without the use of any nails. The picturesque garden features lotus ponds and a quaint hexagonal pavilion. 5 Chi Lin Drive, Diamond Hill, Kowloon 2354 1888 www.chilin.org 09.00–16.30 MTR: Kwun Tong line to Diamond Hill

Kowloon Park

Once a 19th-century military base, the park was redeveloped in 1970 and is now an all-in-one recreational venue. Along with the expected walks and trails, there's an open-air sculpture garden featuring works by both local and overseas sculptors, an aviary, a hedge maze, a Chinese garden and a bird lake with flamingos and other waterfowl. For kids, there's a children's adventure playground, three outdoor pools and an Olympic-size indoor pool. On Sunday afternoons there are free kung fu demonstrations. 22 Austin Road, Tsim Sha Tsui; entrances on Austin Road, Nathan Road, Haiphong Road and Canton Road 2724 3344 www.lcsd.gov.hk 05.00–24.00 MTR: Tsuen Wan to Tsim Sha Tsui

Ladies' Market

This market in Mong Kok specialises in ladies' wear, but you can also find men's and children's clothing. Sizes tend to be on the small side. Accessories such as handbags, shoes, sunglasses, wigs, luggage and watches are also available. Tung Choi Street, stretching from Dundas Street to Argyle Street 12.00–23.30 MTR: Tsuen Wan or Kwun Tong line to Mong Kok

Lei Yue Mun

This charming old fishing village is rapidly modernising, but it still provides a chance to see something authentic before it disappears. You can take the MTR for an afternoon of wandering around the alleyways lined with hundreds of tanks filled with marine life. You can choose dinner from one of these, and the vendor will cook it for you.
ⓐ On the very southern tip of Kowloon in the eastern part of Victoria Harbour ⓝ MTR: Kwun Tong or Tseung Kwan O line to Yau Tong

◉ Clothing and accessories at Ladies' Market

● *Get your fortune told in the Temple Street Night Market*

Temple Street Night Market

Running from about 16.00 until 24.00, this is the liveliest night market in Hong Kong and definitely the place to haggle for a bargain. Set aside the whole evening for your trip to this market, and be prepared to be entertained. As well as shopping for cookware, clothing, sweaters, designer bags and sunglasses, you can have your fortune told by palm readers or astrologers near the Tin Hau Temple. There are street singers who perform Cantonese opera as well as pop songs. What's more, the market is full of *dai pai dong* (licensed mobile food stalls) that specialise in seafood. Finally, it provides a wonderful people-watching opportunity.

ⓐ Temple Street ⓜ MTR: Tsuen Wan line to Jordan

Yuen Po Street Bird Garden

If you spot someone out on the street walking their bird, there's a good chance they bought it at the Bird Garden. The Chinese love birds and there is a multitude of them here squawking, chirping but most of all singing. People mill about buying and selling or simply just admiring the birds in their bamboo cages. It's a great place to take pictures and will provide you with a true Hong Kong experience. ❷ Main entrance facing Boundary Street and another entrance facing Yuen Po Street ❶ 2302 1762 Ⓦ www.lcsd.gov.hk Ⓛ 07.00–20.00 Ⓜ MTR: Tsuen Wan or Kwun Tong line to Prince Edward

CULTURE

Hong Kong Museum of Art

Five permanent galleries showcase a vast collection of ceramics, lacquerware, jade, cloisonné, textiles, wall hangings, scrolls and a great deal more. There are also many special exhibits. To make sure you have

THE SYMPHONY OF LIGHTS

This is a spectacular nightly multimedia event and, according to Guinness World Records, is the world's largest permanent light-and-sound show. It involves more than 30 key buildings on both sides of Victoria Harbour, which are decked in lights that glow in myriad colours when a switch is flicked on. The shows starts at 20.00 and runs for approximately 20 minutes. English narration is on the radio every night on 103.4 FM. Phone ❶ 3566 5665 for more information.

up-to-date information, it's best to check the museum's website.

🅐 10 Salisbury Road, Tsim Sha Tsui 🕿 2721 0116

🕸 www.lcsd.gov.hk 🕒 10.00–18.00 Fri–Wed, closed Thur

Ⓜ MTR: Tsuen Wan line to Tsim Sha Tsui

Hong Kong Museum of History

A showcase of the territory's entire history. The halls documenting the city's modern history, from when it was ceded to the British to the handover, are particularly noteworthy. Look out for the scary yet fascinating map of how much land has been reclaimed in the Victoria

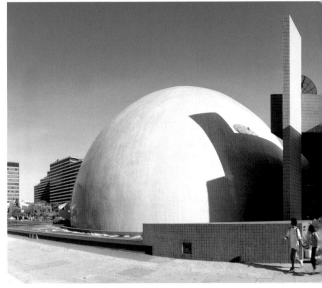

🔺 Let the Hong Kong Space Museum expand your horizons

Harbour area in the last century. ❸ 100 Chatham Road South, Tsim Sha Tsui ☎ 2724 9042 🌐 www.lcsd.gov.hk 🕐 10.00–18.00 Wed–Mon, closed Tues Ⓜ MTR: Tsuen Wan line to Tsim Sha Tsui

Hong Kong Space Museum

Kids love the interactive rides and exhibits along with a Hall of Astronomy and a whole load of information on space exploration. There's a Space Theatre as well, where OMNIMAX films (which provide a full multimedia experience) are shown. ❸ 10 Salisbury Road, Tsim Sha Tsui ☎ 2721 0226 🌐 www.hk.space.museum

🕐 13.00–21.00 Mon, Wed–Fri, 10.00–21.00 Sat & Sun, closed Tues
Ⓝ MTR: Tsuen Wan line to Tsim Sha Tsui

Wong Tai Sin
A very popular Taoist temple, you can wander through halls dedicated to the Buddhist Goddess of Mercy and Confucius. Alternatively, you can throw numbered sticks out of a bamboo container and have your fortune read on the sticks selected. There's also a clinic that advises on both Western and Chinese herbal treatments. ⓐ 2 Wong Tai Sin Estate ⓘ 2327 8141
🕐 07.00–17.30 Ⓝ MTR: Kwun Tong line to Wong Tai Sin

RETAIL THERAPY

Elements Mall An upmarket shopping centre that stands directly above the Kowloon MTR station. Even if you can't afford to splurge on the designer brands housed here, it is worth a visit anyway to check out the artwork and installations gracing the foyers or to have a spin on the ice rink. ⓐ 1 Austin Road West, Tsim Sha Tsui
ⓘ 2735 5234 Ⓦ www.elementshk.com 🕐 10.00–22.00
Ⓝ MTR: Tung Chung line to Kowloon

Golden Computer Arcade With a jumble of shops over several floors offering the latest in electronics goods at extremely competitive prices, this arcade and the adjoining Golden Shopping Centre are a techie's dream. ⓐ 94A Yen Chow Street, Sham Shui Po, Kowloon
🕐 10.00–22.00 Ⓝ MTR: Tsuen Wan line to Sham Shui Po

Granville Road Dozens of clothes stores from standard high-street chains to factory outlets. The cheap threads here are usually overruns

LUCKY JADE & LOVELY PEARLS

Tagged as 'best buys' in Hong Kong, it's a good idea to scoop up a little information about pearls and jade before you set out to purchase. It might even be wise to check out how you can tell real from fake.

The Hong Kong Tourism Board offers advice on purchasing all types of jewellery and watches on its website (ⓦ www.discoverhongkong.com), which includes information on how jade jewellery is classified. Useful contact numbers include The Hong Kong Jewellers & Goldsmiths Association (ⓣ 2543 9633) and The Gemmological Association of Hong Kong (ⓣ 2366 6006).

or pieces that failed quality control, so check everything you buy. Local designer labels and cosmetic stores can also be found here. ⓐ Between Carnarvon Road and Nathan Road ⓒ 11.00–21.00 ⓝ MTR: Tsuen Wan line to Tsim Sha Tsui

Harbour City This is the largest shopping mall in Tsim Sha Tsui and it's easy to get lost, so pick up a map on your way into the centre. There are five interconnecting shopping arcades, including Ocean Terminal and Ocean Centre. ⓐ 5 Canton Road, Tsim Sha Tsui ⓣ 2118 8666 ⓦ www.harbourcity.com.hk ⓒ 10.30–20.00 ⓝ MTR: Tsuen Wan line to Tsim Sha Tsui or take the Star Ferry from Hong Kong Island

Joyce Looking for Prada? This is where you'll find it, along with other top brands, accessories and cosmetics. Joyce has several stores and is a Hong Kong institution. ❸ Harbour City, Canton Road, Tsim Sha Tsui ❶ 2367 8128 ❺ 11.00–21.00 Ⓜ MTR: Tsuen Wan line to Tsim Sha Tsui

Rise Commercial Building Considered a fashion hotspot for those in the know and tucked away from view near the factory outlets in Granville Road. The lesser-known designers are located here, along with boutiques offering unique apparel and accessories from Japan

⬢ Nathan Road is the main thoroughfare in Kowloon

and South Korea. ⓐ 5–11 Granville Road, Tsim Sha Tsui ⓛ 10.30–20.00
Ⓝ MTR: Tsuen Wan line to Tsim Sha Tsui

Winning Commercial Centre Here in this off-the-beaten-track
centre, young, trendy designers have local fashion labels, unusual
imported fashion and second-hand clothing. ⓐ 46–48 Hillwood
Road, Tsim Sha Tsui ⓛ 11.00–20.30 Ⓝ MTR: Tsuen Wan line to
Tsim Sha Tsui

TAKING A BREAK

Kubrick Bookshop Café £ ❶ If you have time to spare before
catching a film at the Cinematheque (where art-house films and re-
runs are screened), you can browse through a good selection of film-
related books and magazines while enjoying a coffee and
sandwiches or pasta. ⓐ 3 Public Square Street, Yau Ma Tei ⓣ 2384
8929 ⓛ 11.30–22.00 Ⓝ MTR: Tsuen Wan or Kwun Tong line to Yau
Ma Tei

Main Street Deli £ ❷ For a quick New-York-style deli lunch in
between shopping bouts, you can get really serious 'deli' here:
hot Reuben sandwiches, latkes, pizza, burgers and so on. The
Deli's other contribution to Hong Kong life is the 'doggy bag'.
ⓐ Langham Hotel, 8 Peking Road, Tsim Sha Tsui ⓣ 2375 1133
ⓦ www.hongkong.langhamhotels.com ⓛ 10.00–22.00
Ⓝ MTR: Tsuen Wan line to Tsim Sha Tsui

Sushi One £ ❸ A conveyor-belt sushi joint with a bustling and
decidedly welcoming atmosphere. ⓐ 23 Ashley Road, Tsim Sha Tsui
ⓣ 2155 0633 ⓛ 12.00–22.00 Ⓝ MTR: Tsuen Wan line to Tsim Sha Tsui

California Pizza Kitchen ££ ❹ This casual, family-friendly eatery features California-style cuisine and pizzas with a twist. Expect international flavours along with unconventional toppings and sauces, and health-conscious options. ➌ 11/F, Shop 10, Megabox, Kowloon Bay ❶ 3421 2351 ⓦ www.cpk.com ⏰ 11.30–24.00 daily Ⓜ MTR: Kwun Tong line to Kowloon Bay

Peninsula Hotel Lobby ££ ❺ This is the city's most famous place for afternoon tea. Nibble on cucumber sandwiches and scones as you listen to live classical music and watch an endless parade of fascinating people going by. ➌ Salisbury Road, Tsim Sha Tsui ❶ 2920 2888 ⓦ www.peninsula.com ⏰ 07.00–24.00 Ⓜ MTR: Tsuen Wan line to Tsim Sha Tsui

Ruby Tuesday ££ ❻ Visit this venue for a major heavy-duty salad bar and large portions for lunch. ➌ Shop Unit P26, Telford Plaza, Kowloon Bay ❶ 2376 3122 ⏰ 11.30–22.30 Ⓜ MTR: Kwun Tong line to Kowloon Bay

AFTER DARK

RESTAURANTS

Khyber Pass Mess Club £ ❼ This popular curry house in the heart of bustling Chungking Mansions serves up authentic Indian and Pakistani dishes. The décor is basic but the dishes famously hot and spicy. ➌ Shop E2, 7/F Chungking Mansions, 36–44 Nathan Road, Tsim Sha Tsui ❶ 2739 1177 ⏰ 12.00–15.30, 18.00–23.30 daily Ⓜ MTR: Tsuen Wan line to Tsim Sha Tsui

A Touch of Spice £–££ ❽ Located in the trendy Knutsford Terrace, A Touch of Spice delivers what its name promises: fragrant Thai and

Vietnamese fare. The sleek-looking yet relaxed dining spot is a perfect place to unwind. ⓐ 1/F, 10 Knutsford Terrace, Tsim Sha Tsui ⓣ 2312 1118 ⓛ 12:00–23:30 daily ⓝ MTR: Tsuen Wan line to Tsim Sha Tsui

Chang Won Korean Restaurant ££ ❾ In Little Korea, this is authentic Korean cuisine, *bulgogi* (a popular beef dish) and all. ⓐ 1/G Kimberley Street, Tsim Sha Tsui ⓣ 2368 4606 ⓛ 11.30–14.30, 17.30–22.30 ⓝ MTR: Tsuen Wan line to Tsim Sha Tsui

Heaven on Earth ££ ❿ Delicious Chinese food with a distinctly home-cooked feel and a penchant towards spice. If the weather's nice, opt for an alfresco dinner, although the retro interior, with its touches of calligraphy, is also pleasant. Try the crispy fried prawns. ⓐ 6 Knutsford Terrace, Tsim Sha Tsui ⓣ 2367 8428 ⓛ 12.00–late Mon–Thur, 16.00–late Fri–Sun ⓝ MTR: Tsuen Wan line to Tsim Sha Tsui

Spring Deer ££ ⓫ This Peking-style eatery has been around for three decades and offers good food for reasonable prices. If your mouth is watering for honey-glazed Peking duck, this is a good place to try it. Excellent hot-and-sour soup, as well as other northern specialities. ⓐ 42 Mody Road, Tsim Sha Tsui ⓣ 2366 4012 ⓛ 11.30–15.00, 18.00–23.00 ⓝ MTR: Tsuen Wan line to Tsim Sha Tsui

Fook Lam Moon £££ ⓬ For almost 50 years, Fook Lam Moon has been serving exotic dishes that are synonymous with Cantonese cuisine – abalone, bird's-nest soup and shark's fin soup – as well as more classic Cantonese choices. A legion of fans claims no other restaurant in Hong Kong does Cantonese so well. ⓐ 53–59 Kimberley Road,

Tsim Sha Tsui ☎ 2366 0286 Ⓦ www.fooklammoon-grp.com Ⓛ 11.30–15.00, 18.00–23.00 Ⓝ MTR: Tsuen Wan line to Tsim Sha Tsui

Megu £££ ⑬ An outpost of the eponymous chic New York restaurant, serving inventive and modern Japanese cuisine. The dishes are beautifully presented but portions are tiny, so leave your appetite at home and come instead for the experience. ⓐ Shop R002–R003, Elements, 1 Austin Road West, Kowloon ☎ 3743 1421 Ⓛ 12.00–15.00, 18.00–23.00 Ⓝ MTR: Tung Chung line to Kowloon

Spoon by Alain Ducasse £££ ⑭ Modern French cuisine by the legendary Michelin-starred chef. Despite the ultra-stylish surroundings, the ambience is not as snobby as you might expect and the service is excellent. Also boasts a stunning harbour view. ⓐ InterContinental Hong Kong, 18 Salisbury Road ☎ 2313 2256 Ⓦ www.hongkong-ic. intercontinental.com Ⓛ 18.00–23.00 Mon–Sat, 12.00–14.30, 18.00–23.00 Sun Ⓝ MTR: Tsuen Wan line to Tsim Sha Tsui

BARS, CLUBS & LIVE PERFORMANCE VENUES

Aqua Spirit Brews with a view are all the rage in Hong Kong, and if the harbour panorama at this bar doesn't bring tears to your eyes, the wallet-squeezing prices will. Good for a sunset tipple before dinner. ⓐ 30th Floor, 1 Peking Road, Tsim Sha Tsui ☎ 3427 2288 Ⓦ www.aqua.com.hk Ⓛ 18.00–01.00 Mon–Thur, 18.00–02.00 Fri & Sat, closed Sun Ⓝ MTR: Tseum Wan line to Tsim Sha Tsui

Bahama Mama's Wrapped in a kitschy Caribbean décor, this bar and dance club has great fruit cocktails and dancing until 04.00. ⓐ 4–5 Knutsford Terrace, Tsim Sha Tsui ☎ 2368 2121 Ⓦ www.mhihk.com Ⓛ 16.00–late Ⓝ MTR: Tsuen Wan line to Tsim Sha Tsui

Balalaika Borrow a fur coat and Russian hat from the friendly staff and down a few shots of vodka in the ice bar, where temperatures are kept, Siberia-like, at -20°C (-4°F). If you get hungry, fill up on some warm *piroshki* (stuffed buns) or freshly grilled *shashlik* (skewers of meat). ❷ 2/F, 10 Knutsford Terrace, Tsim Sha Tsui ☎ 2312 6222 ⏰ 12.00–02.00 Mon–Sat, 18.00–01.00 Sun Ⓝ MTR: Tsuen Wan line to Tsim Sha Tsui

Felix Perched on the top of the Peninsula Hotel, Felix has a view to knock your socks off – just one reason why the chic crowd who patronise the bar insist it's the city's finest venue for drinking. Drinks are expensive, but the atmosphere is heady. ❷ 28th Floor, Peninsula Hotel, Salisbury Road, Tsim Sha Tsui ☎ 2366 6251 Ⓦ www.peninsula.com ⏰ 18.00–02.00 Ⓝ MTR: Tsuen Wan line to Tsim Sha Tsui

Hong Kong Cultural Centre The territory's premier arts venue and home to both the Hong Kong Philharmonic Orchestra and the Hong Kong Chinese Orchestra. Most of the opera and ballet is staged in a 2,100-seat Grand Theatre. There are other smaller concert halls. On Thursday evenings and Saturday afternoons, free live performances take place in the foyer and forecourt. ❸ 10 Salisbury Road, Tsim Sha Tsui ☎ 2734 9009 Ⓦ www.hkculturalcentre.gov.hk Ⓝ MTR: Tsuen Wan line to Tsim Sha Tsui

Lobby Lounge Try one of the lounge's 'Nine Dragons' cocktails as you take in the view of Victoria Harbour and Hong Kong Island. Great spot to watch the Symphony of Lights laser show, which takes place nightly for 20 minutes from 20.00. ❸ InterContinental Hong Kong, 18 Salisbury Road, Tsim Sha Tsui ☎ 2721 1211 Ⓦ www.hongkong-ic.intercontinental.com ⏰ 08.00–02.00 Ⓝ MTR: Tsuen Wan line to Tsim Sha Tsui

New Territories

The New Territories extend from Boundary Street in Kowloon to the Shum Chun River and are a dramatically beautiful panorama of mountain ranges and valleys behind a rugged coastline.

While the New Territories and the Outer Islands make up 90 per cent of Hong Kong's land mass, they have limited facilities compared to Kowloon and Hong Kong Island. Much of this large land area has been gobbled up for housing estates and industrial development, but enough park land still remains to make the New Territories excellent hiking terrain.

Since there have been small settlements and villages here for hundreds of years, it is possible to see remnants of life in days of yore on a day trip via bus or train. For a glimpse of modern-day living, explore one of the many public housing estates, sampling a local meal, visiting the town centre and seeing the residents going about their daily routines.

The New Territories are also home to the Sha Tin Racecourse (see page 34), where race days are held most weekends from September till June.

RAIL TRAVEL IN THE NEW TERRITORIES

Using public transport systems will make your travel in the New Territories much easier and more enjoyable. Ticketing information, maps and schedules for the various systems are available from Hong Kong MTR (see page 54) and **Kowloon–Canton Railway (KCR)** (Ⓦ www.kcrc.com), also known as the MTR's East Rail and West Rail lines.
ⓘ An Octopus Card will make your rail journeys cheaper (see page 60).

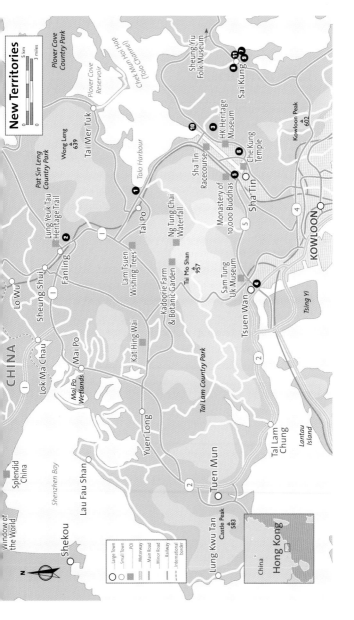

SIGHTS & ATTRACTIONS

Che Kung Temple

This Taoist temple is dedicated to a Sung dynasty general who was deified for his devotion to the villagers of Tin Sam. The general suppressed a revolt in southern China and safeguarded villagers from the plague. Don't leave without turning one of the brass windmills in the courtyard for good luck. ⓐ 7 Che Kung Miu Road, Tai Wai ❶ 3718 6888 ❶ 07.00–18.00 Ⓝ MTR: Ma On Shan line to Che Kung Temple

Hong Kong Heritage Museum

With the exception perhaps of hiking the mountain trails, this is the best reason to come to the New Territories. It is one of Hong Kong's finest museums and a must-see for anyone interested in the history of the region. The Cantonese Opera Heritage Hall is the best place to start. Displays document the changes in how people have lived throughout the centuries. There are ceramics, bronzes, art, furniture and wonderful pieces of jade. For kids, there's a toy museum and a hands-on discovery gallery. ⓐ 1 Man Lam Road, Tai Wai ❶ 2180 8188 Ⓦ www.heritagemuseum.gov.hk ❶ 10.00–18.00 Wed–Mon, closed Tues Ⓝ MTR: Ma On Shan line to Che Kung Temple

Lam Tsuen Wishing Trees

In the village of Lam Tsuen, you can visit a group of giant banyan trees to burn joss sticks and incense paper to make your wishes come true. ⓐ Lam Tsuen village Ⓝ MTR: East Rail line to Tai Po Market, then take bus 64K to the village

◆ *Making offerings at a shrine*

THE MONASTERY OF 10,000 BUDDHAS

In Sha Tin, the temple sits at the top of a wooded hill accessed via a path lined with golden, scarlet-lipped Buddhas. It's a 400-step climb, but you will be rewarded by the sight of the tiny Buddha statues lining the walls (there are actually about 13,000), each one different. The temple was established by a monk named Yuet Kai, now embalmed, covered in gold leaf and placed in a glass case. ⓐ Sha Tin, New Territories ⓣ 2691 1067 ⓦ www.10kbuddhas.org ⓛ 09.00–17.30 ⓝ MTR: East Rail line to Sha Tin, then walk towards Grand Central Plaza

Lung Yeuk Tau Heritage Trail

The trail takes walkers through almost a dozen centuries-old villages, five of which are enclosed within stout walls for safety reasons. Most are connected with the Tang clan, one of the historic Five Great Clans of the New Territories. Information on the trail can be picked up at the Hong Kong Tourism Board's Visitor Information & Services Centres. The HKTB also has maps and a hiking/wildlife guidebook plus other recommended hikes on ⓦ www.discoverhongkong.com ⓝ MTR: East Rail line to Fanling, then take bus 54K to Lo Wai walled village

Mai Po Wetlands

More than 300 species of birds have been recorded at the wetlands, along with a number of Hong Kong's reptile and mammal species. Access to the wetlands is limited, but WWF Hong Kong organises guided public visits all year round. Registration is necessary and can be done online at their website. ⓣ 2526 4473 ⓦ www.wwf.org.hk

Sam Tung Uk Museum

Until a few years ago, members of the Chan clan lived in this 18th-century village and carried on with their daily lives. When the last person left, it was turned into a museum. Four of the houses have been restored to their original condition and furnished with traditional Chinese furniture. ⓐ 2 Kwu Uk Lane, Tsuen Wan ⓘ 2411 2001 Ⓦ www.heritagemuseum.gov.hk Ⓒ 10.00–18.00 Wed–Mon, closed Tues Ⓜ MTR: Tsuen Wan line to Tsuen Wan

◭ *Breathtaking hiking scenery*

Sheung Yiu Folk Museum

This is a good glimpse into Hakka life in the remains of a fortified village built in the 19th century. You can see household goods and belongings along with farm equipment. ❸ Pak Tam Chung Nature Trail, Sai Kung ❶ 2792 6365 ❿ www.heritagemuseum.gov.hk ❹ 09.00–16.00 Wed–Mon, closed Tues ❷ Bus: 94 from the Pak Tam Chung Bus Terminus

RETAIL THERAPY

New Town Plaza A huge shopping and entertainment complex where the locals shop. Features over 300 local and international brands, a gaming arcade, a cinema and a small Snoopy's World theme park for the little ones. ❸ Sha Tin Centre Street, Sha Tin

⬥ Traditional dress in the New Territories

☎ 2699 5992 Ⓦ www.newtownplaza.com.hk 🕐 10.00–22.00
Ⓜ MTR: East Rail line to Sha Tin

Tai Po Megamall This is a group of shopping centres in the Tai Po district which is less crowded than New Town and easily accessible by bus. Ⓐ Tai Po, New Territories Ⓦ www.taipomegamall.shkp.com.hk
Ⓜ MTR: East Rail line to Tai Po Market, then MTR feeder bus K12

TAKING A BREAK

Chung Shing Thai Curry House £ ❶ This is part of a strip of restaurants, but judging by the popularity of this curry house, it may be the best. The curried crab is highly recommended. Ⓐ 69 Tai Mei Tuk Village, Tin Kok Road, Tai Po ☎ 2664 5218 🕐 09.00–24.00 Ⓜ MTR: East Rail line to Tai Po Market

Fung Ying Seen Koon £ ❷ After hiking the Lung Yeuk Tau Heritage Trail, this provides a vegetarian lunch at low cost with lots of imaginative dishes made from mushrooms and bean curd. Ⓐ 66 Pak Wo Road, Fanling ☎ 2669 9186 Ⓦ www.fysk.org 🕐 11.00–17.00 Ⓜ MTR: East Rail line to Fanling

Maxim's Palace Chinese Restaurant £ ❸ The Sha Tin branch of the perennially crowded City Hall Maxim's Palace. A large restaurant with the usual Cantonese dishes plus *dim sum*, seafood and Peking duck. Ⓐ New Town Plaza, Sha Tin ☎ 2693 6918
🕐 07.30–23.45 Ⓜ MTR: East Rail line to Sha Tin

Olive Café & Bar £ ❹ For European-style pasta, pizza and coffee in the heart of Tsuen Wan, head to one of Olive's two locations at either City Landmark or Grand City Plaza, just five to ten minutes from Tsuen Wan MTR station. ⓐ Shop 41–44, G/F, City Landmark 1, 68 Chung On Street, Tsuen Wan ⓣ 2940 6272 ⓦ www.olivecafe.com.hk ⓛ 11.30–23.30 daily ⓜ MTR: Tsuen Wan line to Tsuen Wan

Pho24 £ ⓢ The perfect spot to savour a bowl of *pho* (Vietnamese noodles in a fragrant broth), from which this Hong Kong franchise of Vietnam's world-famous noodle chain takes its name. ⓐ Shop 127, New Town Plaza, Phase 1, 18 Centre Street, Sha Tin ⓣ 2681 2200 ⓛ 11.30–23.00 daily ⓜ MTR: East Rail line to Sha Tin

⬥ *Fast food as an art form*

Royal Park Chinese Restaurant £ ❻ Cantonese food with good *dim sum* at weekends. ⓐ 2nd Floor, Royal Park Hotel, 8 Pak Hok Ting Street, Sha Tin ❶ 2601 2111 ❷ 11.30–14.30, 18.00–22.00 ❷ MTR: East Rail line to Sha Tin

Tung Kee Restaurant £ ❼ This is typical alfresco dining on the waterfront in Hong Kong with junks in the harbour and fishermen offering their catch. ⓐ 96–102 Man Nin Street, Sai Kung (from Hoi Pong Square in the town centre, walk towards the waterfront and turn right) ❶ 2792 7453 ❷ 10.00–22.00

Anthony's Catch ££ ❽ A full-service Italian seafood restaurant with ultra-fresh fish served in huge portions and a great Sunday brunch that features such foreign delicacies as waffles with maple syrup. ⓐ Ground Floor, 1826B Po Tung Road, Sai Kung (from Hoi Pong Square in Sai Kung town centre, walk away from the waterfront along Man Nin Street) ❶ 2792 8474 ⓦ www.anthonyscatch.com ❷ 18.00–22.00 Sun–Thur, 18.00–23.00 Fri & Sat, also open for lunch Sun

Chuen Kee Seafood Restaurant ££ ❾ There are a number of seafood restaurants to sample along the waterfront, but this is a good bet where you can select your dinner from a tank and then have it deliciously prepared. ⓐ 51 Hoi Pong Street, Sai Kung (from Hoi Pong Square in Sai Kung town centre, walk towards the waterfront) ❶ 2791 1195 ❷ 10.00–23.00

Lung Wah Hotel ££ ❿ This restaurant is straight out of a B-movie set and a little difficult to get to. It is famous for its roasted squab (pigeons), which are served with a side dish of greens, with bamboo shoots and mushrooms, and warm towels for your hands.

22 Ha Wo Che, Sha Tin ☎ 2691 1594 ⏱ 12.00–22.00 Ⓜ MTR: East Rail line to Sha Tin, then walk along the railway line toward Ikea

Sauce ££ ⓫ Delicious European fare with outdoor seating. Good value. ⓐ 9 Sha Tsui Path, Sai Kung (take the small lane leading southwest from Hoi Pong Square in Sai Kung town centre) ☎ 2791 2348 ⏱ 11.00–23.00

PUBS & BARS

Aqua Plus A hot new addition to the Sai Kung bar scene, Aqua Plus is attracting plenty of buzz after dark. A warm welcome is guaranteed thanks to its veteran bar managers. ⓐ 72–74 Po Tung Road, Sai Kung ☎ 2791 2030 ⏱ 12.00–late daily

Duke of York Located opposite the bus terminal, the Duke of York is a busy pub serving up great grub in a great atmosphere. Quiz nights, live music and free pool are big draws at this maritime-themed pub catering largely to the expat crowd living in Sai Kung, plus weekenders swapping the city smog for Sai Kung's hiking trails. ⓐ 42–56 Fuk Man Road, Sai Kung ☎ 2791 6255 ⏱ 12.00–late daily

Steamers A sports bar with a good selection of beers and wines plus a decent menu, not just pub stuff. Also does excellent cocktails. ⓐ 66 Yi Chung Street, Sai Kung (from Hoi Pong Square in Sai Kung town centre, walk away from the waterfront along Man Nin Street; Yi Chun Street is a left turn) ☎ 2792 6991 ⏱ 09.00–late

● *View over Cheung Chau and the Outer Islands*

OUT OF TOWN
trips

The Outer Islands

For Hong Kongers, the Outer Islands mean escape from congested city life, plus a chance to dine on seafood by the seaside and frolic on the beaches. The three most favoured islands by visitors to Hong Kong are Cheung Chau, Lamma and Lantau. That said, there are a few others, each with a particular charm. Peng Chau, for example, is much smaller than 'the big three' and has a lovely little village that sells locally made pottery.

GETTING THERE

By water

Regular ferry services ply between Hong Kong and the Outer Islands, leaving early in the morning and returning in the evening. The ferries are cheap, comfortable and usually air-conditioned. Try to avoid taking ferries at weekends if you can, because they are busy and crowded with locals heading to the islands. Some reliable operators:

Hong Kong and Kowloon Ferry (ⓘ 2815 6063 ⓦ www.hkkf.com.hk) serves Lamma and Cheung Chau, and has a customer service centre at Pier 4, Outlying Islands ferry pier.

New World First Ferry (ⓘ 2131 8181 ⓦ www.nwff.com.hk) has a service centre at Pier 6, Outlying Islands ferry pier. Ferries sail to Cheung Chau, Mui Wo (on Lantau) and Peng Chau.

Watertours (ⓘ 2926 3868 ⓦ www.watertours.com.hk) has a whole variety of tours and cruises including to the Outer Islands. The rides are generally from 35 to 50 minutes long.

If you are on a limited schedule, there are organised tours with **HKKF Travel** (ⓘ 2533 5339 ⓔ info@hkkf.com.hk) to Cheung Chau and Lamma.

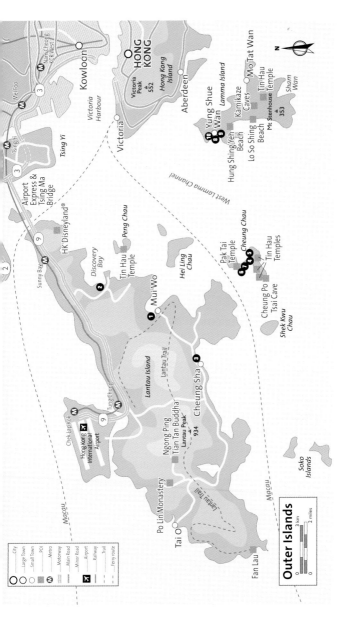

LANTAU

This is Hong Kong's largest island and the first one visitors see, since they land here at Hong Kong International Airport. About 100,000 people live on Lantau, compared to Hong Kong Island's 1.3 million – even though Lantau is twice as big. There is a sizeable expat community clustered in the residential development of Discovery Bay on the northeastern part of the island, where a number of upmarket yet casual restaurants offer alfresco dining.

More than half the island is a designated park, so there are excellent mountain trails including the 70-km (44-mile) Lantau Trail, which passes over Lantau and Sunset Peaks. The famous Tian Tan Buddha is here, plus Po Lin Monastery along with good beaches including Cheung Sha, the longest in Hong Kong.

SIGHTS & ATTRACTIONS
Fan Lau
Fan Lau Fort was built in 1729 to guard the channel from pirates, and a nearby stone circle dates back to the Neolithic or Bronze Age. The only way to reach Fan Lau is on foot from Tai O (walk south from the bus station for 250 m (820 ft) then pick up stage No 7 of the coastal Lantau Trail for about 8 km/5 miles) ⓐ Fan Lau, Lantau ⓦ www.lcsd.gov.hk

Hong Kong Disneyland®
Fantasyland, Adventureland and Tomorrowland executed in a Chinese setting. The 126-ha (311-acre) theme park was opened in late 2005 and is still a hot attraction, particularly for locals and mainland tourists. It's much smaller than other Disneyland® parks, but still a fun day out for the kids. Every evening at around 19.30, there is a fireworks display in front of Sleeping Beauty's

⏶ *Goddesses surround the giant Tian Tan Buddha*

castle. ⓐ Hong Kong Disneyland® Park, Lantau ⓣ 1-830-830
ⓦ park.hongkongdisneyland.com ⓛ 10.30–19.30 ⓝ MTR: Tung Chung
line to Sunny Bay, then board the dedicated train for Disneyland® –
its Mickey-shaped windows are hard to miss

Po Lin Monastery

This huge Buddhist monastery and temple complex was built in
1924 and attracts many visitors, both because of its location near
the giant Buddha and also for its simple vegetarian restaurant –
good, inexpensive and substantial food that's definitely worth
sampling. Known as the Buddhist Kingdom in the South, the
monastery ranks first for structure among the four most popular
Buddhist temples in Hong Kong. You can stay overnight in the
temple if you want to catch the sunrise on the Fong Wong Shan
Mountain the next morning. ⓐ Ngong Ping, Po Lin (follow the
directions for the Tian Tin Buddha, see opposite) ⓣ 2985 5248
ⓦ www.plm.org.hk ⓛ 09.00–18.00

Tai O

One of the more interesting trips on the island is a visit to Tai O,
a Tanka village on the west coast that used to be an important
trading port with China. Today, it is a place where visitors come
to ride a rope-tow ferry pulled mostly by elderly Hakka women,
to walk around the village watching merchants processing salt
fish or to visit some of the workshops of resident craftspeople.
Traditional houses still stand in the centre of the village and you
can get a glimpse of the seafaring past on the waterfront where
some of the village's famous stilt houses still remain. ⓐ Tai O village,
Lantau ⓝ Ferry from Central Pier 6 to Mui Wo, then bus 1 to Tai O,
MTR Tung Chung station, then bus 11 from Tung Chung town centre

WHERE WHITE DOLPHINS ARE PINK

Think of a marine animal made of bubble gum and that's pretty much the colour of these Chinese white dolphins, which can be seen in the coastal waters off Lantau (if you're very lucky). Now threatened by environmental pollution, these once abundant dolphins are down in numbers to between 100 and 200. There has been a lot of controversy about the whole situation, including protests that the natural coastline of Lantau Island was eroded during land reclamation and the construction of Hong Kong International Airport. Sewage dumping, overfishing, chemical dumping and boat traffic all take their toll, not to mention fishing that often traps the dolphins in nets.

For more information and organised dolphin-watching cruises, contact **Hong Kong Dolphin Watch** (ⓣ 2984 1414 ⓦ www.hkdolphinwatch.com).

Tian Tan Buddha

Situated on the Ngong Ping plateau at an elevation of 738 m (about 2,400 ft), this Buddha is so huge you'll have your first glimpse of it while on the bus en route. Clocking in at more than 30 m (98 ft) and weighing 250 tonnes, it's the world's largest seated outdoor bronze Buddha and can be seen from as far away as Macau on a clear day. Make sure you're fit because there are more than 260 steps up to the Buddha, but the climb is well worth it. It's a dramatic photo for shutter bugs. ⓐ Ngong Ping, Po Lin ⓣ 2985 5248 ⓦ www.plm.org.hk ⓛ 09.00–18.00 ⓝ From Silvermine Bay, take the bus 2 bound for Ngong Ping. Make sure you have the exact fare of HK$16 (weekdays)

or HK\$25 (Sundays) or use the handy Octopus Card (see page 60).
The ride from Silvermine Bay takes about 45 minutes. You can also
catch the dramatic Ngong Ping Cable Car from Tung Chung, which
takes 25 minutes and costs from HK\$107 for a round trip.
Ⓦ www.np360.com.hk

TAKING A BREAK

Bahce £ ❶ A small restaurant serving Turkish food such as
stuffed vine leaves and filo pastry filled with cheese plus the
usual falafel and kebabs. ❷ 3 Ngan Wan Road, Mui Wo Centre,
Mui Wo (Silvermine Bay) ❶ 2984 0222 ● 11.30–23.00 Ⓝ Take the
ferry to Mui Wo from Central Ferry Pier 6

D Deck £–££ ❷ A collection of alfresco cafés and restaurants on
the waterfront in Discovery Bay. Choose from a quick sandwich
or kebab to fresh seafood, Korean barbecue or traditional Sichuan.
❶ 3851 2345 Ⓦ www.ddeck.com.hk ● 09.00–22.00 Ⓝ Take the ferry
to Discovery Bay from Central Ferry Pier 3

Stoep ££ ❸ A beautiful location right on the beach with food
served alfresco. Barbecued meats cooked South Africa style are
a speciality, but there are other continental dishes and a good
wine list. ❷ 32 Lower Cheung Sha Village ❶ 2980 2699 or 9465
● 10.00–22.00 Ⓝ Take the ferry to Mui Wo from Central Ferry Pier 6,
then bus 4 to Cheung Sha Beach

AFTER DARK

Bars

China Beach Club Pleasant rooftop bar and open-air balcony
overlooking Silvermine Bay Beach. Good food. ❷ 18 Tung Wan Tau

● The waterfront at Tai O

Road 🕿 2983 8931 🕐 12.00–22.00 (happy hour all day Thur–Sat)
Ⓝ Take the ferry to Mui Wo from Central Ferry Pier 6

China Bear This is a good place to relax with a microbrew or one of
a long list of fine beers before leaving Lantau since it is close to the
ferry pier and bus terminal. ❷ Mui Wo Centre, Mui Wo 🕿 2984 9720
🕐 10.00–02.00 Ⓝ Take the ferry to Mui Wo from Central Ferry Pier 6

CHEUNG CHAU

At one time, the residents of Cheung Chau were full-time fishermen
and part-time pirates who did a little smuggling on the side. The island,
after all, was perfectly located to prey on passing ships. One of the
more famous pirates, Cheung Po Tsai, made a base on the island and
you can still visit the cave in which he allegedly stowed his booty.

The island has a few beaches and windsurfing is a highly popular
pastime. It also proudly boasts that a native son won the gold medal
in windsurfing in the 1996 Atlanta Olympics. Even though the island
is only 2.5 sq km (about 270,000 sq ft), it supports a population of
about 30,000, many of these commuters who work on Hong Kong
Island or Kowloon. To explore Cheung Chau, pick up a map and
ferry schedules from the HKTB website (see page 152). Ferries leave
from Central Ferry Pier 5. There is no public transport on Cheung Chau,
but there are bicycle rental shops near the ferry pier.

SIGHTS & ATTRACTIONS
Beaches
There are a number of good beaches on the island, but one of the
best is Tung Wan on the eastern end of Tung Wan Road. It's a large
beach by Hong Kong standards and a good, safe place to swim.

Shark nets are up during the swimming season, which is May to October. Other beaches include those at Tai Kwai Wan and Tung Wan Tsai on the northern end.

Cheung Po Tsai Cave

On the southwestern peninsula, this cave was allegedly the favourite hiding place of the notorious pirate Cheung Po Tsai. It is a 2-km (just over 1-mile) walk from Cheung Chau village along Sai Wan Road. The pirate, who once commanded a flotilla of 600 junks and had a private army of 4,000 men, surrendered to the Qing government in 1810 and became a bureaucrat. Rumour insists that his treasure still lies buried somewhere on the island.

CULTURE
Pak Tai Temple

This is the oldest and most famous temple on the island and dates back to 1783. Guarded by two stone lions, it is dedicated to the Taoist deity Pak Tai whom legend says spared the island's residents from the plague when it was decimating other islands in the area. As the god of the sea, Pak Tai protects fishermen. Inside, there's an iron sword measuring 1.5 m (5 ft) in length that was found by local fishermen and thought to be 1,000 years old. However, the temple is most famous as the focal point of the annual Cheung Chau Bun Festival (see page 11), and inside the temple is a sedan chair in which Pak Tai's statue is carried during the event.

Tin Hau Temples

Since Tin Hau was the empress of heaven and the patroness of seafarers, it's not surprising that there are four temples on the island dedicated to this deity: the Pak She Tin Hau Temple is about 100 m (330 ft)

northwest of the Pak Tai Temple; Nam Tan Wan Tin Hau Temple is just north of Morning Beach; Tai Shek Hau Tin Hau Temple is to the west of Sai Wan Road; Sai Wan Tin Hau Temple is west of Western Bay.

TAKING A BREAK
Restaurants
Hometown Teahouse £ ❹ After a day on Tung Wan Beach, this relaxed place with a terrace run by a likeable Japanese couple is perfect for lunch or dinner. They also serve afternoon tea Japanese style, which means sushi, pancakes and tea. ❷ 12 Tung Wan Road ❶ 2981 5038 ❸ 12.00–24.00

Bayview Chinese Restaurant ££ ❺ Sweeping views of the South China Sea, sumptuous seafood and local Cantonese fare, all freshly prepared. ❸ Warwick Hotel, Tung Wan Beach ❶ 2981 0081 ❿ www.warwickhotel.com.hk ❸ 07.00–14.30, 18.00–21.00

Hong Kee ££ ❻ Along with a number of other restaurants, Hong Kee is famous for its lobster with black bean sauce. ❷ Ground Floor, 11A Pak She Praya Road ❶ 2981 9916 ❸ 11.30–22.00

New Baccarat Seafood Restaurant ££ ❼ One of the oldest of the many restaurants crowding the waterfront, it has seating under a canopy and specialises in seafood. Try their garlic deep-fried prawns. ❷ 9A Pak She Praya Street ❶ 2981 0606 ❸ 11.00–22.30

Bars & pubs
Lai Kan's This is a Cheung Chau institution and is named after the owner, although it's also known as the Patio Café. As an open-air café with a pub, it's attached to the Windsurfing Centre at Tung Wan

⬤ The Bun Festival offers such spectacles as floating children!

Beach. **ⓐ** Cheung Chau Windsurfing Centre, 1 Hak Pai Road
ⓣ 2981 8316 **ⓛ** 12.00–19.00

Morocco's Bar & Restaurant On the waterfront, this was a favourite
drinking spot when there was a large expat community living on
Cheung Chau. It's still a good place to have a beer and enjoy some
decent Indian food served by the friendly owners. **ⓐ** 117 Praya Street
ⓣ 2986 9767 **ⓛ** 10.00–03.00

LAMMA

As the closest of the Outer Islands (about 25 to 35 minutes by fast
and ordinary ferry), Lamma is also Hong Kong's third-largest island,
with a population of about 12,000.

It's still largely undeveloped with no cars on the island but a
great place for hiking on a 90-minute Family Trail that links the
island's two villages. The hike has some great ocean views as well as
glimpses of Ocean Park and Aberdeen on Hong Kong Island. The
smaller of the two villages, Sok Kwu Wan, is the place to go for
alfresco seafood. The larger, Yung Shue Wan, has a population of
young bohemian foreign residents, which is its big draw. The island
also has some good beaches, including **Lo So Shing Beach**, the most
beautiful on the island.

If you're planning a day visit to Lamma, take the ferry to Sok Kwu
Wan and stop to enjoy a delicious seafood lunch before hiking to a
nearby beach. From there, you can take the trail to Yung Shue Wan
for dinner before heading back to Central. Ferry services are more
frequent to this town than Sok Kwu Wan and leave for Lamma from
Central Ferry Pier 4. There are also smaller ferries – with a more local
flavour – between Aberdeen pier and Mo Tat Wan.

SIGHTS & ATTRACTIONS

Kamikaze Caves

On the eastern shore, these caves were constructed by the occupying Japanese forces during World War II and were designed to hide small speedboats packed with explosives that would be used in suicide attacks on Allied shipping. The war ended before they could be used and the caves have since been allowed to

BEACHES

Hung Shing Yeh Lamma's most popular beach, but to avoid the crowds try to come during the week. There are toilets and changing rooms and shark nets to protect bathers.

🅐 Approximately 25 minutes by foot southeast from Yung Shue Wan ferry pier

Lo So Shing South of Hung Shing Yeh and below a Chinese Pavilion on the path. While not big, this is the most beautiful beach on the island and it does have trees for shade.

🅐 Approximately 20 minutes by foot west from Sok Kwu Wan ferry pier

Mo Tat Wan A clean and relatively uncrowded beach but has no lifeguards. 🅐 Approximately 30 minutes by foot east from Sok Kwu Wan ferry pier, or accessible by ferry from Aberdeen pier

Sham Wan Another beautiful bay, and is considered the best and most secluded beach. To get here, you have to follow a narrow overgrown track. This is the only beach in Hong Kong where green turtles still lay their eggs in the nesting season (June–October) and the beach is closed then. 🅐 Approximately 40 minutes by foot southeast from Sok Kwu Wan ferry pier

deteriorate and be reclaimed by nature. ❷ A ten-minute walk south from Sok Kwu Wan ferry pier, past the Tin Hau Temple

Mount Stenhouse

For climbers, this 353-m (1,158-ft)-high mountain has spectacular views from the summit over all of Lamma and beyond to Hong Kong and Lantau islands. The route up is a tough scramble on a rocky path but worth the struggle. ❷ Approximately 30 minutes by foot south from Sok Kwu Wan ferry pier to the base

TAKING A BREAK

Blue Bird £ ❶ An unadorned little spot with basic but tasty Japanese dishes and good sushi and sashimi. ❷ 24 Main Street, Yung Shue Wan ❸ 2982 0687 ❹ 11.30–15.00, 17.30–00.30

The Bookworm Café £ ❶ Everything is vegetarian and organic (try the fruit juices and organic wine) and there's a good range of food, from breakfasts to burgers, falafels and pizzas. Best of all, it's downright

⬥ *The tranquillity of Lamma*

inexpensive. It has its name because there's a second-hand bookshop here as well as an Internet café. 🅐 79 Main Street, Yung Shue Wan 🅣 2982 4838 🅦 www.bookwormcafe.com.hk 🅛 10.00–21.00

Sampan Seafood Restaurant ££ ⑩ This restaurant is popular with locals for seafood and pigeon dishes, as well as *dim sum*. 🅐 16 Main Street, Yung Shue Wan 🅣 2982 2388 🅛 07.00–22.00

Pubs

The Deli-Lamma In keeping with its hip name, this place with its terrace on the harbour caters to a hip crowd in the evening. There's on-tap cider and basic pub fare. 🅐 36 Main Street, Yung Shue Wan 🅣 2982 1583 🅛 09.00–late

Diesel's Sports Bar A favourite hangout of the expat community, this place is crammed full on Saturday nights with cheering football and rugby fans. 🅐 51 Main Street, Yung Shue Wan 🅣 2982 4116 🅛 18.00–late

Further afield (Macau & Shenzhen)

Macau and Shenzhen – quite different though they are – both exert a strong cultural fascination. The former spent almost half a millennium as a Portuguese colony and is now styled the Las Vegas of the East; the latter, which was a nondescript town less than a generation ago, is now China's richest city per head of population.

GETTING THERE

By air

Sky Shuttle (☎ 2108 9898 🌐 www.skyshuttlehk.com) has a helicopter shuttle to Macau from the helipad on top of the ferry terminal. The flight takes 16 minutes between Hong Kong and Macau.

By rail

The most comfortable way to go to Shenzhen is via KCR East Rail from East Tsim Sha Tsui station. Trains leave from around 05.30 to 24.00. The journey from East TST station to the border takes about 40 minutes.

By road

From Hong Kong, you'll find buses to Shenzhen run by a host of companies that leave from various points at different times during the day. Two companies to check out are **CTS Express Coach** (☎ 2365 0118 🌐 http://ctsbus.hkcts.com) and **Eternal East Cross Border Coach** (☎ 3412 6677 🌐 www.eebus.com).

By water

Most people take the ferry from Hong Kong to Macau. **New World First Ferry** (☎ 2131 8181 🌐 www.nwff.com.hk) has high-speed

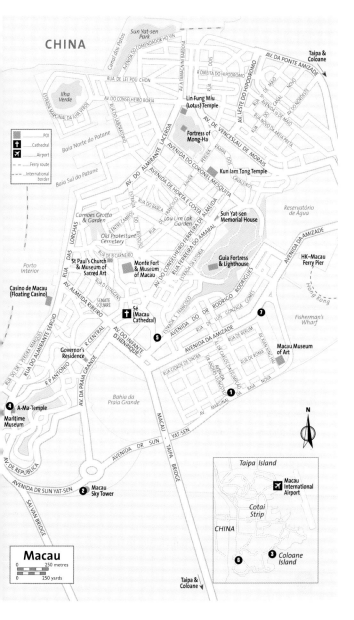

catamarans from Tsim Sha Tsui with departures on the half-hour from 07.00 to 24.00. The trip takes between 65 and 75 minutes and tickets start at HK$133. **TurboJet** (☎ 2859 3333 🌐 www.turbojet.com.hk) has regular crossings that take between 55 and 65 minutes from Hong Kong to the ferry terminal in Macau. The company also operates both jetfoils and catamarans. High-speed jetfoils run from **Macau Ferry Terminal** (✏ 200 Connaught Road on Hong Kong Island) between the two territories every 15 minutes.

MACAU

Much was made of the political handover of Hong Kong to China in 1997 after more than 150 years of British rule, but Macau was a Portuguese colony for 450 years before it was returned to Chinese hands in 1999. As the first and last major European colony in Asia, little wonder that it remains one of the most hybrid places on earth, culturally swinging back and forth between Chinese and Portuguese.

Once you get past the Las Vegas-style casinos and mega resorts you will find a charming fusion of Asian and Mediterranean, whether it's in the architecture, churches, food, temperaments or lifestyle.

Pastel-coloured churches sit on cobblestone streets which are identified on blue-and-white *azulejos* (Portuguese enamel tiles) near Buddhist and Taoist temples. In town, Chinese stores are jumbled with colonial-style buildings, and shopkeepers blend Chinese practicality with Portuguese warmth and flair. Macau is also unashamedly remodelling itself as a glamorous gambling destination, with big international names like Las Vegas Sands and Wynn Resorts opening casinos here. Macau's Cotai Strip, inspired by the Las Vegas Strip, is where you will find most of the new resorts.

◆ *The Lou Lim Lok Garden*

A day trip or an overnight stay in Macau are appealing for several reasons: there seems to be something for everyone here. There are a number of special things to do in Macau, like trying your luck at the horse or dog races. Alternatively, you can people-watch at the 24-hour-a-day floating casino. Take an evening stroll along Macau's **Fisherman's Wharf** (Ⓦ www.fishermanswharf.com.mo) to browse through souvenir shops, the amusement park and man-made volcano. Then, even if you've already bungee jumped off it, end your day watching the sun set from Macau's own 'space needle'.

There are temples, gardens, fortresses, beaches, excellent museums, historical treasures and casinos. Hotels tend to be cheaper and, as a duty-free port with lots of new, smart boutiques, Macau is a mecca for shopping. Since the Macau peninsula is only 1.5 km (1 mile) wide and 4.75 km (3 miles) long, you can walk to most of the sights. However, there are taxis (painted black and beige) that are inexpensive.

SIGHTS & ATTRACTIONS
Camoes Grotto & Garden
He likely didn't live in Macau, but Portugal's famous 16th-century poet Luis Vaz de Camoes has always been much loved here. Locals convinced that Camoes made the journey to the East say that he composed one of his most famous works here, *The Lusiads*. A bust of the poet sits in the centre of the park. Just to the right of the garden, the restored Old Protestant Cemetery has some interesting 19th-century graves of European and American Protestants who lived in Macau. ❷ Praca Luis de Camoes, 15-minute walk northwest from Senate Square ❶ 06.00–23.30

Lou Lim Lok Garden
A wealthy 19th-century Chinese merchant enchanted with the famous gardens in Suzhou, China, created this replica for his own

and posterity's pleasure. There are narrow winding paths, a zigzag bridge to deter bad spirits, carp pools, rock grottos and bamboo groves. A peaceful place, even more so in the morning when local tai chi practitioners are going through their exercises and bird lovers, with their birds, fill the garden with song. ⓐ Estrada de Adolfo Loureiro ① 2835 6622 ⓛ 06.00–18.00 ⓝ Bus: 12, 17, 18, 19, 22 or 23

Macau Sky Tower

This broadcasting tower is where you'll find an observation deck with amazing panoramic views and some of the most daredevil adventure activities this side of Asia, including bungee jumping, a mast climb and a hands-free walk around the outer rim of the tower. ⓐ Largo da Torre de Macau ① 2893 3339 ⓦ www.macautower.com.mo ⓛ 10.00–21.00 Mon–Fri, 09.00–21.00 Sat & Sun ⓝ Bus: 9A, 18, 23 or 32

Monte Fort

For history buffs, the Monte Fort overlooking St Paul's was built by the Jesuits in the early 17th century and is the site of the city's most famous battle, in 1622. At the time the fort was guarded by a small force of African slaves, soldiers and priests, one of whom fired a lucky shot that landed in the powder supply of the invading Dutch ships and drove them back. From this point you'll find a great view of most of Macau on a clear day. ⓐ Monte Fort, a ten-minute walk north from Senate Square ⓦ www.macautourism.gov.mo ⓛ 10.00–18.00

St Paul's Church

On a visit here, photo buffs invariably head to St Paul's Church following the mosaic tiles from Macau's main colonial-era square to the striking ornate façade of the church, all that remains of the once powerful cathedral. Originally built in 1602, the church caught

◆ *The grand staircase and façade of St Paul's Church*

fire during a typhoon in 1835 and burnt to the ground. Walking up the grand staircase leading to the façade, you can understand why historians call this the finest monument to Christianity in Asia.

ⓐ Rua do Belchior Carneiro, a ten-minute walk north from Senate Square ⓦ www.macautourism.gov.mo

Sun Yat-sen Memorial House

Sun Yat-sen is widely recognised by Chinese people everywhere as being the modern founder of their country. This was once the home of Dr Sun Yat-sen's first wife and it contains a collection of flags, photos and other memorabilia. ⓐ Avenida Sidonio Pais ⓣ 2857 4064 ⓛ 10.00–17.00 ⓝ Bus: 12, 17, 18, 19, 22 or 23

CULTURE

Macau Museum of Art

A small museum displaying historical paintings, contemporary local artists, Chinese calligraphy, pottery and other interesting bits and bobs. ⓐ Avenida Xian Xing Hai ⓣ 8791 9882 ⓦ www.artmuseum.gov.mo ⓛ 10.00–18.30 Tues–Sun, closed Mon ⓝ Bus: 1A, 8, 12, 17 or 23

Museum of Macau

This museum in the ancient Monte Fort has an excellent overview of Macau's history, its traditions and its art. Displays include paintings and photos showing Macau through the centuries, a peek at its architecture and cuisine, and a comparison of the Chinese and European civilisations at the time of their encounter in the 16th century. There are interesting comparisons between the two writing systems of the cultures, their philosophies and religions. A re-created street scene lined with colonial and Chinese shop façades is well done. ⓐ Citadel of Sao Paulo do Monte, a ten-minute walk north from

Senate Square ☎ 2835 7911 ⓦ www.macaumuseum.gov.mo
🕐 10.00–18.00 Tues–Sun, closed Mon

Temple of Kun Iam Tong

Dedicated to the Goddess of Mercy, this is one of the most important
temples in Macau and is well worth a visit. The temple was founded
in the 13th century, but most of its buildings date from 1627. A statue
of Kun Iam, who is dressed like a bride, is attended by 18 golden figures
on the walls that represent the 18 wise men of China. In the same
room, you'll see an odd statue with bulging eyes that is supposed
to represent Marco Polo. In the garden behind the temple, there are
four intertwined banyan trees known as Lovers' Trees because they
symbolise marital fidelity. Local legend says that they grew from the
graves of two lovers who committed suicide. ⓐ Avenida do Coronel
Mesquita 🕐 07.00–18.00 ⓝ Bus: 12, 17, 18, 19, 22 or 23

RETAIL THERAPY

Things tend to be cheaper here than in Hong Kong, so while the
choices may not be as plentiful, the prices are better. The most popular
purchases are curios, furniture and antiques. Some furniture and

---

SPECIAL TREATS

Soak up a bit of art history with rotating shows in a gallery
called the Leal Senado. Or do a little shopping along the Avenida
do Infante Dom Henrique or the Avenida de Almeida Ribeiro,
the main shopping areas. Antiques on Rua de Sao Paulo, Rua
de Sao Antonio and Rua das Estalagens are especially good,
as well as collector item stamps at the main post office.

antique shops offer an overseas shipping service. There are many dealers who will claim that the item they are trying to sell you is authentically antique. But it may not be – reproductions from China are everywhere. Some of the more reputable shops can be found on Rua de Sao Paulo. Knitwear is another popular buy in Macau, since the territory manufactures woollen and cotton garments. If you shop around, you can pick up seconds, discontinued lines or overruns of popular labels for a song. Electrical goods, gold jewellery and Chinese herbs and medicine are also popular.

TAKING A BREAK

One of the best reasons to visit Macau is for a taste of the subtle blending of Chinese and Portuguese flavours known as Macanese cuisine. Being world explorers, the Portuguese brought spices from Africa, codfish and vegetables from Europe, chillis from India, and sweet potatoes, kidney beans and peanuts from Brazil. These are used in a dish called *feijoada* – a stew of pork, black beans, cabbage and spicy sausage that is washed down with a young wine called *vinho verde*. Here are some great places to eat, day or night.

Antica Trattoria da Isa £ ❶ In the nightlife district, this restaurant is always crowded, but its 18 different kinds of pizza are great, as are other traditional Italian dishes. ❸ Edificio Vista Magnifica Court 40–46, Avenida Sir Anders Ljungstedt ❶ 2875 5102 ❷ 12.00–15.00, 18.00–23.00 ❷ Bus: 1A, 8, 12, 17 or 23 down Avenida Dr Sun Yat-sen

360° Cafe ££ ❷ A revolving restaurant at the top of the Macau Sky Tower serving a smorgasbord of cuisines, from traditional Portuguese to continental grills. The selection may not be as wide as gourmands may like, but the food is good and the city views

⬥ *Macau's food traditions are quite different to Hong Kong's*

stunning. ⓐ Macau Tower, Largo da Torre de Macau, off Avenida Dr Sun Yat-sen ⓣ 8988 8622 ⓦ www.macautower.com.mo
ⓛ 11.30–15.00, 18.30–22.00 ⓝ Bus: 9A, 18, 23 or 32

Fernando's ££ ❸ This brick building on the beach with a pavilion is the best for atmosphere and authentic food. The menu is strictly Portuguese with Fernando, the owner, doing wonderful things with codfish, chicken, pork ribs, suckling pig, prawns, mussels and so on. They bake their own bread and stock only Portuguese wine. ⓐ Praia de Hac Sa 9, Coloane Island ⓣ 2888 2531 ⓛ 12.00–21.30 ⓝ Bus: 15, 21A, 25 or 26A

A Lorcha ££ ❹ Some of the best Portuguese food in Macau, the dishes to sample here are *piri piri*, *feijoada* and *porco balichao*

tamarino. ❷ Rua do Almirante Sérgio 289A ❶ 2831 3193 ❸ 12.30–15.00, 18.30–23.00 Wed–Mon, closed Tues Ⓝ Bus: 1, 1A, 2, 5, 6, 7, 9, 10A, 11, 18, 21, 21A, 28B or 34

Clube Militar de Macau ££–£££ ❺ For a special night out, this is excellent Macanese/Portuguese cuisine in an atmospheric setting. For lunch, there's a first-class buffet complemented by the best wine list in town. ❷ Avenida da Praia Garande 795, a five-minute walk southeast from Senate Square ❶ 2871 4000 ❸ 11.30–15.00, 18.00–23.00

Espaco Lisboa £££ ❻ This tiny two-storey restaurant is known for its traditional, country-style Portuguese food with mouth-watering fried codfish cakes, sautéed clams in garlic and coriander and Portuguese cabbage soup just for starters. One of the best finds in Coloane Village. ❷ Rua das Gaivotas 8, Coloane Village, Coloane Island ❶ 2888 2226 ❸ 12.00–15.00, 18.30–22.00 Mon–Fri, 12.00–22.30 Sat & Sun Ⓝ Bus: 15, 21A, 25, 26 or 26A

> **TWO FOR THE PRICE OF ONE**
>
> To sample the special Macanese blending of these two cultures, the **Nga Tim Café** (❶ 2888 2086) on the main square of Coloane Village is an inexpensive but delicious place for lunch. While in the village (and after trying Coloane's two beaches), a couple of good dining spots are Espaco Lisboa (see above) for gourmet Portuguese, and Fernando's (see opposite) for moderately priced Portuguese seafood dishes served on a patio on the beach.

Naam £££ ❼ The décor is great, the Thai food is sublime –
everything you'd expect from a Mandarin Hotel. ⓐ Ground Floor,
Mandarin Oriental Hotel, Avenida da Amizade 956–110 ❶ 8793 4818
ⓦ www.mandarinoriental.com ❶ 12.00–14.30, 18.30–22.30
ⓝ Bus: 1A, 3, 3A, 10, 10A, 10B, 11, 12, 17, 23, 28A, 28B, 28C or 32

AFTER DARK

Macau was once the nightlife sin centre for Asia, with opium dens and
lots of intrigue. Things have changed but it's wise to avoid the tacky
floorshows and hostess clubs, and to check with Macau Tourism for
recommendations. Macau Fisherman's Wharf is a safe bet and there
are trendy discos on Avenida do Infante D Henrique.

Pubs & clubs

There are pubs and clubs in great abundance in Macau, especially in
the NAPE, an area of reclaimed land, and inside some of the newer
casinos. Theme bars line the waterfront and some have live music.

Casablanca Café This is an elegant spot with cool jazz in the background
and photos of Hollywood and Hong Kong film stars decorating the
walls. ⓐ Vista Magnifica Court Building, Avenida Dr Sun Yat-sen,
Macau Peninsula ❶ 2875 1281 ❶ 17.30–03.00 ⓝ Bus: 1A, 8, 12, 17 or 23

Signal Café A very popular spot with young locals in the waterfront
area. ⓐ Avenida Dr Sun Yat-sen ❶ 2875 1052 ❶ 11.30–23.00 ⓝ Bus: 1A,
8, 12, 17 or 23

Vasco A live band and a small dance floor that fills up as the
night wears on. Probably the classiest watering hole in Macau.
ⓐ Mandarin Oriental Hotel, 956-110 Avenida da Amizade ❶ 8793 3831

Ⓦ www.mandarinoriental.com Ⓛ 12.00–14.30, 18.30–22.30 Ⓜ Bus: 1A, 3, 3A, 10, 10A, 10B, 11, 12, 17, 23, 28A, 28B, 28C or 32

Performing arts

Macau Cultural Centre The city's main venue for classical music concerts, dance performances and studio film screenings. Ⓐ Avenida Xian Xing Hai Ⓣ 2870 0699 Ⓦ www.ccm.gov.mo

Ⓘ The Macau Government Tourist Office (MGTO) also publishes a free monthly guide – *Macau Travel Talk* – that lists what's going on. It is available at most large hotels and MGTO offices.

ACCOMMODATION

For overnight stays, there are many hotels and glitzy, Las Vegas-style resorts, from the expensive **Four Seasons** (Ⓐ Cotai Strip, Taipa Ⓣ 2881 8888 Ⓦ www.fourseasons.com/macau) to the moderately priced **Pousade de Coloane** (Ⓐ Praia de Cheoc Van, Coloane Island Ⓣ 2888 2144 Ⓦ www.hotelpcoloane.com.mo), a small, family-owned property on a hill above Cheoc Van Beach.

SHENZHEN

Shenzhen, the Special Economic Zone (see page 136) that straddles the Hong Kong border to the north, is China's richest city per head and was one of the People's Republic of China's five original SEZs.

Less than 30 years ago, it was a little town with a population of 20,000. Today, its population exceeds 12 million and it has a distinct boomtown aura. (For location, see map on pages 52–3.)

Shenzhen has its own stock exchange, traffic congestion and skyscrapers sitting cheek by jowl. It also has pollution. But most

of all, it beckons to anyone wanting an even better bargain than in Hong Kong. Come here to have clothing made, shop for real bargains, have a massage or manicure, or just get a glimpse into where China is going without going to Beijing. Shenzhen prides itself on being one of China's most cosmopolitan cities, so no matter where you go you will hear dialects and accents from all over the country.

You will need a visa to enter Shenzhen. This is available either at the border or in Hong Kong (see page 142). Getting it at the border limits you to five to seven days within the confines of Shenzhen SEZ. It's recommended that you pay the extra and get a proper Chinese visa that will allow you to visit other places in China and also avoid a horrendous queue at the border.

SIGHTS & ATTRACTIONS
Diwang Mansion
One of Shenzhen's tallest skyscrapers at 69 floors, there's a viewing platform on the 68th floor with a good panorama of the city and some of Hong Kong. ② 5002 Shennan Road East, Futian District ⏰ 09.30–16.30 Ⓝ Metro: Line 1 to Guomao

> ### SPECIAL ECONOMIC ZONES
> Special Economic Zones (SEZs) were developed by the People's Republic of China to encourage foreign investment in China, and to bring much-needed jobs, technical knowledge and future tax revenues in return for significant tax concessions at start-up. They are not unlike SEZs in other parts of the world and include cities in the provinces of Guangdong, Fujian, Hainan, Hunchun and Pudong (Shanghai).

◆ *Traditional ways persist in Shenzhen, China's richest city*

Shenzhen Lychee Park

A large, tranquil park and lake with arched bridges that are fun for photo ops. Named after its numerous lychee trees. Keep an eye out for the rehearsing ballroom dancers strutting their stuff out in the open air. HongLing Middle Road, Futian District 05.00–24.00 Metro: Line 1 to Dajuyuan

Splendid China

This is a theme park with miniatures of China's most historic buildings and sites, including the Temple of Confucius, the Great Wall of China and the Imperial Palace. Shenzhen Bay 2660 0626 10.00–19.00 Metro: Line 1 to Shijiezhichuang

Window of the World

Taking a global look, the world's most famous monuments are here squeezed into 480,000 sq m (0.2 sq miles). The 108-m (354-ft)-tall Eiffel Tower dominates the skyline, and the sight of the Pyramids and the Taj Mahal in such close proximity is part of the slightly kitsch appeal of this theme park. Additionally, there's a wide selection of international restaurants and mini exhibitions on famous figures from world history. You can eat Mexican food, see the Niagara Falls, then wander around Angkor Wat. The site takes at least half a day to explore and every day ends with a firework and laser show. Shenzhen Bay 2755 2690 10.00–20.00 Metro: Line 1 to Shijiezhichuang

RETAIL THERAPY

Shopping is the raison d'être behind most day visits to Shenzhen because prices for quality goods are lower than in Hong Kong and bargainers can drive a harder bargain – sometimes reducing the price by as much as 75 per cent.

⬥ *See the world at Window of the World*

Hua Qiang Bei Lu This is one of the newer shopping areas in the heart of the city with rows and rows of small shops similar to Lowu Commercial City. Ⓜ Metro: Line 1 to Huaqianglu

⬤ *Shenzhen is a shopper's delight*

Lowu Commercial City A huge centre with 1,500 small shops that offer more variety in goods than anywhere else in Shenzhen. Head up to the Fabric Mall on the fifth floor for a custom-made suit or dress, or take a look at the shoe and handbag shops. It is usually very busy; avoid obvious scams and keep an eye on belongings. On the second floor, stalls sell freshwater pearls, jade, beads and semiprecious stones. ❷ The first shopping centre you'll see coming out of the immigration control point if you take the overland train from Hong Kong

MiXc A swish shopping centre in downtown Shenzhen with designer boutiques, a supermarket, a cinema and an ice rink. Also houses a range of fast-food restaurants and cafés. ❷ Shennan Middle Road Ⓦ www.themixc.com ❶ 10.00–22.00 Ⓜ Metro: Line 1 to Dajuyuan

TAKING A BREAK
Noodle King £ If there's little time left over after running from shop to shop, this is a good stop for a quick lunch of dumplings, noodles and vegetable dishes. ❷ 3021 Renmin Nanlu, a ten-minute walk northeast from Lowu station ❶ 8222 2348 ❶ 11.30–21.30

Summer Tea House £ It may have an unprepossessing interior, but this vegetarian restaurant serves up some tasty food, including a wide range of mock meat dishes. ❷ 7F Jin Tang Building, 3038 Baonan Lu ❶ 2558 6555 ❶ 12.00–15.00, 17.30–21.00 Ⓜ Metro: Line 1 to Guomao

Ocean King Restaurant ££–£££ The best place in Shenzhen for seafood – always popular and packed. ❷ 1116 Jianshe Lu, a ten-minute walk northwest from Lowu station ❶ 8223 9000 ❶ 12.00–14.30, 18.00–21.30

Bars & pubs

360° Bar, Restaurant and Lounge Located in the Shangri-La Hotel, this is a comfortable and stylish place for an after-shopping drink. ⓐ 1002 Jianshe Lu, a ten-minute walk northwest from Lowu station ⓣ 8233 0888 ⓦ www.shangri-la.com ⓛ 17.00–02.00

THE REST OF CHINA

China is such a vast country with so much to see that an 'extension' after a Hong Kong trip can only be a taste of what another trip could offer. Try to decide what appeals to you most – a cultural or historical experience, shopping, seeing the most famous sights or an adventure.

For culture, Yunnan and Sichuan introduce the many minority ethnic groups with their special customs and costumes. For history, there's Xian with its amazing terracotta warriors or the fabulous bronzes of Sanxingdui. Shanghai can't be beaten as a shopping experience, with Beijing close behind, adding as a bonus the Great Wall. For an adventure, there are caravans to the vast northwestern deserts or the highest train ride in the world to the Tibetan plateau.

All China trips require a visa. Obtaining one of these can take from one to three days. You'll need two photos, which you can get at one of the photo booths in the MTR (see page 54). ⓐ Visa Office of the People's Republic of China, 7th floor, Lower Block, China Resources Centre, 26 Harbour Road, Wan Chai

● *Slick and modern: Hong Kong International Airport*

PRACTICAL
information

Directory

GETTING THERE

By air

As the major gateway to China, Southeast Asia and much of the East, more than 85 international airlines operate between Hong Kong International Airport and 150 other destinations worldwide. Hong Kong-based **Cathay Pacific** (Ⓦ www.cathaypacific.com) flies nonstop to most major international airports.

From the UK, the major airlines flying direct to Hong Kong are:
British Airways ❶ 0844 493 0787 Ⓦ www.ba.com
Qantas ❶ 0845 774 7767 Ⓦ www.qantas.co.uk
Virgin Atlantic ❶ 0844 209 7777 Ⓦ www.virgin-atlantic.com

For direct flights from North America, try:
Air Canada ❶ 1 888 247 2262 Ⓦ www.aircanada.ca
American Airlines ❶ 1 800 433 7300 Ⓦ www.aa.com
Continental Airlines ❶ 1 800 231 0856 Ⓦ www.continental.com

If you're travelling from Australia or New Zealand, airlines that offer nonstop flights include:
Air New Zealand ❶ 0800 737 000 Ⓦ www.airnewzealand.com
Qantas ❶ 13 13 13 Ⓦ www.qantas.com.au

Many people are aware that air travel emits CO_2, which contributes to climate change. You may be interested in the possibility of lessening the environmental impact of your flight through the charity **Climate Care** (Ⓦ www.jpmorganclimatecare.com), which offsets your CO_2 by funding environmental projects around the world.

ENTRY FORMALITIES

Citizens of the UK, Republic of Ireland, other EU countries, the USA, Canada, Australia, New Zealand and South Africa must hold a valid passport extending at least six months after your planned departure date from Hong Kong. Nationals of most countries do not need visas for visits of up to 90 days.

Hong Kong may be a duty-free port, but there are certain items on which duty is charged – for example, alcohol (100 per cent on spirits, but 0 per cent on wine and beer). You can bring in duty-free 60 cigarettes and one litre of alcohol. Apart from this, most things are permitted with the exception of firecrackers and fireworks and, of course, drugs.

MONEY

The Hong Kong dollar (HK$) is made up of 100 cents. Coins are: bronze-coloured 10 cents, 20 cents and 50 cents; silver HK$1, HK$2 and HK$5; nickel and bronze HK$10. Denominations of notes are: HK$10, HK$20, HK$50, HK$500 and HK$1,000.

As a major financial centre, Hong Kong has no currency controls, which means you can bring in or send out as much money as you want. When changing money, banks usually offer the best rates, although the major banks levy a commission. The city has many licensed moneychangers, such as Chequepoint (especially in the tourist areas), and while these are open at convenient hours (for example, Sundays, late in the evening), they offer less attractive exchange rates than the banks. ATMs can be found almost everywhere and are linked to most international money systems such as Plus, Cirrus and Maestro. The most widely accepted credit cards are Visa, MasterCard, American Express, Diners Club and JCB. Although the credit card companies forbid it, some shops may try to add a surcharge for credit cards. When signing credit card receipts, make sure you always write 'HK' in front of the dollar sign if it's not already there.

HEALTH, SAFETY & CRIME

As with most Asian countries, the major risk for travellers is stomach upsets caused by eating contaminated food, or drinking contaminated water. Drink only bottled water (ensure the seal has not been broken) or water that has been boiled for at least three minutes. Stay away from ice, raw food, unpasteurised milk and milk products, and raw shellfish, which has been linked to hepatitis outbreaks. Fears that you shouldn't eat chicken or other poultry because of avian flu are unwarranted – the city government moved quickly to cull infected birds and is keeping stringent checks on the situation.

For its size, Hong Kong is a remarkably safe city, but stick to well-lit areas if walking around at night. Police officers patrol frequently, especially in the Tsim Sha Tsui area, and they are helpful to visitors. To avoid hassles, exercise the usual common-sense safety rules such as locking up your valuables in a safe, keeping an eye on belongings in crowded areas and being wary of people offering gambling or investment opportunities.

Hong Kong has world-class hospitals providing outstanding care, but the service is expensive so travel insurance is vital. In the case of an emergency, an ambulance will take you to a government-run public hospital where you will have to pay a large sum for emergency services. Treatment is guaranteed, so even if you can't pay immediately you can be billed later.

OPENING HOURS

Generally, business hours are weekdays 09.00–17.00 and Saturdays 09.00–13.00. Major banks are open weekdays 09.00–16.30 and

Saturdays 09.00–12.20. They are closed Sundays and public holidays. The vast majority of shops are open every day 10.00–19.00. Stores in busy retail areas like Wan Chai, Causeway Bay and Tsim Sha Tsui stay open as late as 21.30. Museums are usually open six days a week 09.00–17.00 with one day closed (usually Monday or Tuesday).

TOILETS

In the past, Hong Kong has been annoyingly short of public toilets, but this is rapidly changing. New ones are being built and old ones upgraded with baby-changing tables in both men's and women's toilets and good facilities for those with disabilities.

It's usually free to use these toilets, but keep tissues on hand because toilet paper quickly runs out. Restrooms in hotels and restaurants are usually the best bet as far as cleanliness goes.

CHILDREN

Hong Kong is generally a child-friendly place, although babies and toddlers might find the hot and muggy weather challenging. Foreign children still tend to attract attention from locals, particularly if they're blonde and blue-eyed. Fascinated strangers might want to touch or hold your baby – if you're not comfortable with this, just smile and back away.

Children are normally welcome in casual restaurants and eateries, and supermarkets and pharmacies readily stock baby food and products.

Adults may find Hong Kong a shopper's paradise, but kids are not forgotten when it comes to attractions.

The Mid-Levels Escalator (see page 46) is free and great fun. The longest escalator in the world, it consists of three moving walkways and 20 elevated escalators, and was built as an unusual but practical form of transport for residents living in the upper levels. It's an interesting 20-minute experience, and you can get on and off to check out great shops and restaurants along the way so adults don't get bored too quickly.

If you're looking for more colour, the Yuen Po Street Bird Garden (see page 83) has various courtyards filled with trees and stalls selling birds and cages and with lots of non-caged birds swooping around.

⬤ *The Mid-Autumn Festival is one of Hong Kong's most important festivals*

Hong Kong also has several theme parks to keep the young ones entertained, including Hong Kong Disneyland® (see pages 108 & 110) and Ocean Park (see page 66), which has a cable-car ride, Dragon roller coaster and the stomach-churning Abyss turbo prop ride, plus marine animal shows and much more.

For an educational experience, take your kids down to the Hong Kong Heritage Museum (see page 96). Just southwest of Sha Tin town centre, this museum looks like an ancestral hall. As well as its large collection of arts, it has a wonderful children's discovery gallery. Here, kids can peek into Hong Kong life or check out the Cantonese Opera Heritage Hall where they can make themselves up as Cantonese opera characters on a computer.

The Hong Kong Space Museum (see pages 85–6) is another favourite. Located on Salisbury Road, this venue has one of the largest planetariums in the world, a Space Theatre with OMNIMAX films, plus treasures such as a rocket-ship model, NASA's 1962 *Mercury* space capsule and Moon rocks.

For more ideas, download HKTB's *Hong Kong Family Fun Guide* at Ⓦ www.discoverhongkong.com. Most of the admission fees and transport services are half-price for kids under 12 years of age.

COMMUNICATIONS
Internet

Broadband access in Hong Kong is widespread and should be available at your hostel or hotel. If you suddenly need to get online while you're out and about, Internet cafés, while not on every street corner, are possible to find. Your best bet is one of the **Pacific Coffee Company** (Ⓦ www.pacificcoffee.com) outlets, which have terminals for patrons to use.

Phone

Hong Kong uses an eight-digit system and provides clear-sounding connections. The country code is 852. To get an English-speaking operator for directory assistance, dial 1081. Phone rates are cheaper from 21.00 to 08.00 on weekdays and throughout the weekend.

TELEPHONING HONG KONG

The code for Hong Kong is 852 (for Macau, it's 853).
There are no area codes.

🔴 Please note that, to phone Shenzhen, you need to dial 86, then 755, then the subscriber number

TELEPHONING ABROAD

From Hong Kong, you can make international direct-dial calls from most public telephones with a phonecard (Hello or Smartcards). These are available from 7-Eleven and Circle K convenience stores, Mannings pharmacies, Wellcome supermarkets, PCCW branches and retail outlets.

To place a call to someone outside Hong Kong, dial 001, then the country code, the local area code and the number. When dialling Hong Kong from abroad, drop the initial 0 from the local area code. Some country codes:

Australia 61	**Macau** 853
Canada 1	**Netherlands** 31
China (Mainland) 86	**New Zealand** 64
France 33	**South Africa** 27
Germany 49	**United Kingdom** 44
Japan 81	**United States** 1

If the phone you are using has the facility, dial 0060 first and then the number – rates will be cheaper at any time.

Public payphones cost HK$1 for five minutes. Phones accept HK$1, HK$2, HK$5 and HK$10 coins. All local calls from private phones are free, but hotels will charge between HK$3 and HK$5 for local calls.

Hong Kong has the world's highest per capita usage of mobile phones, and they work everywhere, including in tunnels and on the MTR. Hong Kong mobile services operate on the same technology as most European countries (GSM and W-CDMA), so check with your operator to see if you can receive roaming services here.

Post

With its British roots, the Hong Kong postal service is excellent – with letters often being delivered the same day they are sent in the city. International airmail is divided into two zones: Zone 1 includes China, Japan, Taiwan, South Korea, SE Asia and Indonesia; Zone 2 is everywhere else. Airmail generally takes from three to eight days. Rates start at HK$2.40 (under 20 grams) for Zone 1 and HK$3 for Zone 2. Local mail is HK$1.40 for up to 30 grams. Aerogrammes are a uniform HK$2.30.

General Post Office (on Hong Kong Island) ➋ 2 Connaught Place, Central District 🕓 08.00–18.00 Mon–Sat, 09.00–17.00 Sun

Tsim Sha Tsui Post Office (Kowloon) ➋ Ground Floor, Hermes House, 10 Middle Road 🕓 08.00–18.00 Mon–Sat, 09.00–14.00 Sun

Postal boxes are lime-green on lavender pillars, all clearly marked in English. Staff at the post offices speak English and there is Saturday delivery. ☎ 2921 2222

ELECTRICITY

Electrical current is 220 volts, 50 cycles alternating current (AC). Plugs can be confusing, though. While most take the British three square pins, some will take three large round prongs and others three small pins. Inexpensive plug adaptors are available in many stores and supermarkets.

For overseas dual voltage appliances, be sure to bring a converter and an adaptor. Blackouts and other electrical catastrophes are generally rare in Hong Kong.

TRAVELLERS WITH DISABILITIES

Because of its geography, Hong Kong is not the easiest city in the world for people with disabilities. Rail and underground stations have stairs, footpaths tend to be crowded, and there are many steep hills. Newer venues such as the airport and Hong Kong Convention & Exhibition Centre do have facilities for wheelchairs and most have lifts with Braille panels. Wheelchairs can also negotiate the lower decks of most ferries and some buses are wheelchair accessible.

The huge airport has moving walkways as well as ramps and lifts. There are no special taxis for the disabled, but drivers do carry walking aids such as wheelchairs and crutches.

For more information on services for travellers with disabilities, contact:

Hong Kong Paralympic Committee & Sports Association for the Physically Disabled Ⓦ www.hkparalympic.org

Joint Council for the Physically and Mentally Disabled
Ⓦ www.hkcss.org.hk

TOURIST INFORMATION

Hong Kong Tourism Board The HKTB bends over backwards to be helpful, has a large willing staff and heaps of literature. The office hotline is open 08.00–18.00 to solve all problems on Ⓣ 2508 1234 or check Ⓦ www.discoverhongkong.com

HKTB Visitor Information & Service Centres These are on Hong Kong Island, in Kowloon, in Hong Kong International Airport on Lantau and in Lo Wu on the border with mainland China. In other parts of Hong Kong, iCyberlink screens are available from which you can access the HKTB website and database 24 hours a day. The free HKTB *Visitor's Kit* gives a description of the city's main tourist attractions and information on shopping. Visitors' hotline: ☎ 2508 1234

Hong Kong International Airport ⓐ Halls A & B on arrivals level and in the E2 transfers area ⏰ 07.00–23.00

Hong Kong Island HKTB Centre ⓐ 99 Queen's Road, Causeway Bay MTR station, near exit F ⏰ 08.00–20.00

Kowloon HKTB Centre ⓐ Star Ferry Concourse, Tsim Sha Tsui ⏰ 08.00–20.00

Lo Wu HKTB Centre ⓐ 2nd Floor, Arrivals Hall, Ko Wu Terminal Building ⏰ 08.00–18.00

Useful websites

Time Out magazine for nightlife and entertainment ⓦ www.timeout.com.hk

Hong Kong Information Services Department ⓦ www.lcsd.gov.hk

BACKGROUND READING

East and West: The Last Governor of Hong Kong on Power, Freedom and the Future by Chris Patten. The politician who oversaw the handover of Hong Kong writes about his experiences in the colony.
Hong Kong: China's New Colony by Stephen Vines. A hard factual examination of the territory after the British left.
Hong Kong: Epilogue to an Empire by Jan Morris. The Welsh travel writer alternates chapters on Hong Kong's history with descriptions of its geography, economy, politics and society.

Emergencies

The following are emergency freephone numbers:

Ambulance/fire/police ☎ 999

Crime hotline ☎ 2527 7177

Lost credit cards American Express ☎ 2811 6122; Diners Club ☎ 2860 1888; MasterCard ☎ 800 966 77; Visa ☎ 800 900 782

In an emergency, dial ☎ 999. Operators speak both English and Cantonese.

Police advise street crime victims to file a report at the nearest police station. The most common complaints from visitors are about being ripped off by shops. The police in Tsim Sha Tsui (☎ 2678 2887) monitor such cases and may be able to help.

Go to the 'Crime Prevention' tab on the Police Force website (ⓦ www.police.gov.hk) for more information.

For lost passports, contact your consulate after notifying the police on ☎ 2860 2000

MEDICAL SERVICES

The Hospital Authority One-Stop Enquiry Service has two 24-hour hotlines (☎ 2882 4866 and 2300 6555) with full information on emergency services. Accident and emergency services are provided 24 hours a day at the hospitals listed below:

Prince of Wales Hospital ◉ 30 Ngan Shing Street, Sha Tin, New Territories ☎ 2632 2211

Matilda Hospital ◉ 41 Mt Kellett Road, The Peak, Hong Kong Island ☎ 2849 0123

Queen Elizabeth Hospital ◉ 30 Gascoigne Road, Kowloon ☎ 2958 8888

Queen Mary Hospital ◉ 102 Pok Fu Lam Road, Hong Kong Island ☎ 2855 3111

EMERGENCY PHRASES

Help!	**Stop!**	**Thief!**	**Fire!**
Gau-meng!	*Káy hái-do!*	*Yáu cháat aa!*	*Fó-jùk aa!*

Call the police!	**Call an ambulance!**
Faai-dì giu gíng-chaat!	*Faai-dì giu gau-sèung-chè!*

POLICE

The Hong Kong Police Force is professional and generally helpful –
not the sort you need to bribe to get anything done. Uniforms are
a light blue shirt with dark blue trousers and blazer.

Hong Kong Island Central Division @ Arsenal House, Police Headquarters,
1 Arsenal Street, Wan Chai ☏ 2543 4603 Ⓜ MTR: Tsuen Wan or Island
line to Admiralty

EMBASSIES & CONSULATES

For a complete list, dial **Directory Assistance** on ☏ 1081

Australian Consulate @ 23rd floor, Harbour Centre, 25 Harbour Road,
Wan Chai ☏ 2827 8881

Canadian Consulate @ 11th–14th floors, Tower One, Exchange Square,
8 Connaught Place, Central ☏ 3719 4700

New Zealand Consulate @ Room 6508, 65th Floor, Central Plaza,
18 Harbour Road, Wan Chai ☏ 2877 4488

South Africa Consulate @ Rooms 2706–2710, 27th floor, Great Eagle
Centre, 23 Harbour Road, Wan Chai ☏ 2577 3279

UK Consulate @ 1 Supreme Court Road, Central ☏ 2901 3000

US Consulate General @ 26 Garden Road, Central ☏ 2523 9011

A

Aberdeen 62
accommodation 36–41
air travel 50–51, 54
arts *see* culture

B

background reading 153
Bank of China Tower 64
bars & clubs 30–32
    see also nightlife
beaches 114–15, 119
beliefs 18–20, 22
birds 67, 83, 98, 148
bus travel 54, 122

C

cafés *see also* restaurants
    Hong Kong Island
        70–72
    Kowloon 89–90
Camoes Grotto
    & Garden 126
Cantonese Opera
    Heritage Hall 48
car hire 60
Causeway Bay 25, 62
Central 62
Che Kung Temple 96
Cheung Chau 114–16, 118
Cheung Po Tsai Cave 115
Chi Lin Nunnery 80
children 147–9
China 142
Chinese medicine 22
cinema 32–3, 100, 141
crime 141, 146, 154
culture 20–22, 115–16
currency 145–6
customs & duty 145

D

dim sum 28–9
designer labels 68
disabilities, travellers
    with 147, 152

Diwang Mansion 136
dolphins 111

E

EA Experience 66
electricity 151–2
embassies &
    consulates 155
emergencies 154–5
entertainment 30, 32–3
    see also nightlife
etiquette 29
events 8–15

F

Fan Lau 108
feng shui 18–19, 64
ferries 54, 60, 106, 114,
    118, 122, 124
festivals 8–15
Fisherman's Wharf 126
Flagstaff House Museum
    of Tea Ware 67
food & drink 26–9
Forever Blooming
    Bauhinia 64
Fringe Club 76

G

Golden Bauhinia
    Square 64

H

health 22, 146, 154
helicopters 122
history 16–17
Hollywood Road 70
Hong Kong Academy of
    Performing Arts 76
Hong Kong Convention
    & Exhibition Centre 76
Hong Kong
    Cultural Centre 93
Hong Kong
    Disneyland® 108, 110
Hong Kong Heritage
    Museum 96, 149

Hong Kong Island 62–77
Hong Kong Museum
    of Art 83–4
Hong Kong Museum
    of History 84–5
Hong Kong Space
    Museum 85–6, 149
hospitals 146, 154
horse racing 34
hotels *see*
    accommodation

I

International Dragon
    Boat Festival 14–15
internet 149

J

jade 87
Jumbo Kingdom 66

K

Kadoorie Farm &
    Botanic Garden 46
Kamikaze Caves 119–20
Kowloon 55, 78–93
Kowloon Park 80

L

Ladies' Market 80
Lam Tsuen
    Wishing Trees 96
Lamma 118–21
Lan Kwai Fong (LKF) 30, 62
Lanes, The 70
Lantau 108–14
Lei Yue Mun 81
lifestyle 18–19
listings 32
Lock Cha Tea Shop 48
Lou Lim Lok Garden 126–7
Lung Yeuk Tau
    Heritage Trail 98

M

Macau 122–35
Macau Cultural Centre 135

Macau Museum of Art 129
Macau Sky Tower 127
Madame Tussauds 66
Mass Transit Railway 58, 60
Mai Po Wetlands 98
Man Mo Temple 67–8
markets 25, 78, 80, 82
Mid-Levels Escalator 46, 147–8
Monastery of 10,000 Buddhas 98
money 145–6
Mong Kok 78
Monte Fort 127
Mount Stenhouse 120
Museum of Macau 129–30
music 30, 32–3, 74, 76–7, 135

N
New Territories 55, 58, 94–104
Ng Tung Chai Waterfall 46
nightlife 30, 32–3
    Hong Kong Island 74, 76–7
    Kowloon 92–3
    Macau 134–5
    New Territories 104
    Shenzhen 142

O
Ocean Park 66, 149
Octopus Card 60
opening hours 146–7
Outer Islands 58, 106–21

P
Pacific Place 70
Pak Tai Temple 115
passports & visas 136, 142, 145

pearls 87
phones 150–51
Po Lin Monastery 110
police 146, 155
Police Museum 48
post 151
public holidays 13
public transport 58–60, 94, 106, 114, 118, 122, 124
Punchline Comedy Club 30

R
rail travel 54, 58, 94, 122
restaurants 18, 26–9
    Cheung Chau 116
    Hing Kong Island 72–4
    Kowloon 90–92
    Lamma 120–21
    Lantau 112
    Macau 131–4
    New Territories 101–4
    Shenzhen 141

S
safety 55, 146
St Paul's Church 127–9
Sam Tung Uk Museum 99
seasons 8
Sha Tin Racecourse 34, 94
Shenzhen 122, 135–42
Shenzhen Lychee Park 138
Sheung Yiu Folk Museum 100
shopping 24–5, 48–9
    Hong Kong Island 68–70
    Kowloon 86–9
    Macau 130–31
    New Territories 100–101
    Shenzhen 138, 140–41
SoHo 30–2, 62
Special Administrative Region 16–17, 55

Special Economic Zones 136
Splendid China 138
sport & relaxation 34–5
Stanley 62
Stanley Market 25
Star Ferry 45
suits 24
Sun Yat-sen Memorial House 129
symbols & abbreviations 4
Symphony of Lights 47, 83

T
tai chi 35
Tai O 110
taxis 60
tea 48, 67
Temple of Kun Iam Tong 130
Temple Street Night Market 25, 82
theatre 76–7, 93
Tian Tan Buddha 111–12
time difference 50
Tin Hau Temples 115–16
toilets 147
tourist information 152–3
Tsim Sha Tsui 78

V
Victoria Park 35
Victoria Peak 66–7

W
weather 8, 48–9
Window of the World 138
Wong Tai Sin 86

Y
Yau Ma Tei 78
Yuen Po Street Bird Garden 83, 148

Z
Zoological & Botanic Gardens 67

ACKNOWLEDGEMENTS
The publishers would like to thank the following individuals and
organisations for supplying their copyright photographs for this book:
Hong Kong Tourist Board, pages 5, 12, 27, 31, 33, 34, 44, 59, 61, 81, 84–5, 88 &
120–21; Macau Government Tourist Office, pages 125, 128 & 132;
Dreamstime page 10 (Mike Kwok), page 143 (Youssouf Cader); Getty, page
15; Panos, pages 137 & 139; Pictures Colour Library, pages 39, 42–3, 69, 102
& 140; Helena Zukowski, all others.

Project editor: Penny Isaac
Proofreaders: Jan McCann & Kelly Walker
Layout: Trevor Double

Send your thoughts to
books@thomascook.com

- **Found a great bar, club, shop or must-see sight that we don't feature?**
- **Like to tip us off about any information that needs a little updating?**
- **Want to tell us what you love about this handy little guidebook and
  more importantly how we can make it even handier?**

Then here's your chance to tell all! Send us ideas, discoveries and
recommendations today and then look out for your valuable input
in the next edition of this title.

Email the above address (stating the title) or write to:
pocket guides Series Editor, Thomas Cook Publishing, PO Box 227,
Coningsby Road, Peterborough PE3 8SB, UK.

WHAT'S IN YOUR GUIDEBOOK?

Independent authors Impartial up-to-date information from our travel experts who meticulously source local knowledge.

Experience Thomas Cook's 165 years in the travel industry and guidebook publishing enriches every word with expertise you can trust.

Travel know-how Thomas Cook has thousands of staff working around the globe, all living and breathing travel.

Editors Travel-publishing professionals, pulling everything together to craft a perfect blend of words, pictures, maps and design.

You, the traveller We deliver a practical, no-nonsense approach to information, geared to how you really use it.

Useful phrases

English	Cantonese approx pronunciation
BASICS	
Yes	*h<u>a</u>i*
No	*<u>ǹ</u>g•hai*
Please	*ng•gòy ...*
Thank you	*dàw•j<u>e</u> (l<u>á</u>y)*
Hello	*hàa•ló*
Sorry	*deui•<u>ǹ</u>g•j<u>e</u>w*
I don't speak Cantonese	*ng<u>á</u>w <u>ǹ</u>g sik gáwng gwáwng•dùng wáa*
Do you speak English?	*l<u>á</u>y sìk•<u>ǹ</u>g•sìk gáwng yìng•mán aa?*
Good morning	*jó•s<u>à</u>n*
Good afternoon	*<u>ǹ</u>g•ngâwn*
Good evening	*m<u>á</u>an•ngâwn*
My name is ...	*ng<u>á</u>w giu ...*
NUMBERS	
One	*yàt*
Two	*y<u>i</u>*
Three	*s<u>à</u>am*
Four	*say*
Five	*<u>ǹ</u>g*
Six	*l<u>u</u>k*
Seven	*chàt*
Eight	*baat*
Nine	*gáu*
Ten	*s<u>a</u>p*
Twenty	*y<u>i</u>•s<u>a</u>p*
Fifty	*<u>ǹ</u>g•s<u>a</u>p*
One hundred	*yàt•baak*
SIGNS & NOTICES	
Airport	*gay•chèung*
Railway Station	*foh•che•jàam*
Platform	*yuet•tóy*
Smoking/Non-smoking	*sik•yin/<u>ǹ</u>g•ho sik•yin*
Toilet	*chi•sáw*
Ladies/Gentlemen	*n<u>u</u>/n<u>à</u>an*